RAILWAY REFLECTIONS

RAILWAY REFLECTIONS

A unique collection of photographs from the '30s by
F.C. Le Manquais
with a commentary by
Thomas Middlemass

PATRICK STEPHENS LIMITED

British Library Cataloguing in Publication Data

Middlemass, Thomas
Railway Reflections
1. Great Britain. Railway services,
1929–1939
I. Title
385'.0941

ISBN 1-85260-089-6

Patrick Stephens Limited is part of the
Thorsons Publishing Group
Wellingborough, Northamptonshire, NN8 2RQ, England

Printed and bound in Great Britain by Butler & Tanner Ltd, Frome and London

1 3 7 9 10 8 6 4 2

CONTENTS

FOREWORD

BY COLIN GARRATT

This mouth-watering collection of unique images from the 1920s and '30s is remarkable, not only for what it has to tell us about railways during the period, but also for the insight that it offers into social history and transport policies to the present day. These pictures, expertly interpreted by Tom Middlemass, portray the steam age at the very pinnacle of its achievement in the British Isles. The pictures offer an exceptional insight into the most flamboyant period in the evolution of transport and one which remains constantly worthy of study by railway and social historians.

In many ways the 1930s may be regarded as the richest period in locomotive history. Britain's railways, born out of private enterprise, reflected the individualism of the private companies and, quite apart from the incredible diversity of locomotive designs, rolling stock, architecture and operational practice abounded in diversity, much of which remains in evidence to this day. It is in this historic mould that Britain's present day high-tec railway is irretrievably cast. Though this situation causes endless headaches for today's railway operators, it does provide the interested observer with endless fascination. No other modern industry bears the marks of its history as do our railways.

As you study these pictures, note that not only did Le Manquais get around the country by train, but he *could* get around by train and to the most obscure corners of these islands, without the need for an independent internal combustion engine. One of many aspects brought to light by studying the Le Manquais pictures is the simple truth that family motor cars, juggernaut lorries and motorways, are irrelevant to the functioning of a properly co-ordinated transport system. A truth which many adults have long since forgotten—not least our national leaders—whilst to younger generations, the very concept of a railway-based economy is unimaginable.

Yes, there are many lessons to be learned from a study of the pictures and the commentary in this book, not least in the fact that Britain's railways appear to be coming full circle. Not since pre-grouping times have such a variety of liveries and innovations been evident on Britain's railways as they are today. The resurgence of rail traffic, with the stimuli of 'sectorization' and regional financial control, has produced a railway scene of colour and diversity which almost rivals the post-grouping period featured in these photographs. Don't be in any doubt that if Le Manquais were still wielding his camera today, he would be delighting in the development of such great new trains as the 'Sprinter' units and the debut of the Class '91' 'Electra' InterCity 225's on the East Coast main line. The 'Electra' is a potential world-beater, which recalls the flamboyance of Gresley's 'Coronation' of half a century ago. The Channel Tunnel opens up a new epoch of railway potential and diversity, yet despite its advanced technology and potential to compete with airlines for land distances of up to 500 miles, it is but the fulfilment of the railway pioneers' intentions of a century ago—so deep are railways rooted in our industrial development.

I have no hesitation in commending this book to you, confident that there is much to learn from history, for without it, the present has no perspective and the future no meaning.

Colin Garratt
Newton Harcourt
Leicestershire

PREFACE

Any railway enthusiast who lived through the 1930s was a fortunate man indeed. Grouping was firmly established, the spirit of competition was rife, and, with no prescience of either war or rail nationalization looming ahead, he existed in a constant state of railway bliss. The 'Big Four' dominated the railway scene, and for an infinite variety of personal reasons appropriate company allegiances were duly forged. My own was comparatively simple: my father was an old North British Railway goods guard —hence I was an LNER man!

Like many another schoolboy I haunted local stations, and spent the bulk of my leisure time tracking down and recording locomotives: at first names, then, as stockbooks emerged, numbers. Inevitably, within a year or two ambition flowered, the family Box Brownie was wheedled from its hiding place, and my first tentative overtures at railway photography commenced. As the new decade, the 1930s, opened up, it soon became painfully apparent that more sophisticated equipment was required and, anxiously scrutinizing the sales ads in the *Amateur Photographer*, I took a deep breath, wrote to London, and bound myself to twelve monthly instalments of 6/8d. Phew, *four quid* for a camera—and I had only just started work at £30 a year!

There was only one slight snag. When the new camera arrived, so, too, did half a dozen slide holders. It was a plate camera; albeit 3¼in × 2¼in. A cut-film adaptor which also arrived to complicate matters proved singularly clumsy in use and prone to scratching. In despair I summoned up a few more coppers, and invested in a roll-film adaptor. Not the most elegant of alternatives, I fear, but at least it got me on my way. So, eagerly—though, of course, cautiously in modern 35mm terms—I snapped away. Who could help it! New locomotive types were emerging all over the place, particularly in Central Scotland.

It has taken me nearly fifty years, and several subsequent cameras, to appreciate fully the error of my adolescent ways. Nowadays I show a typical young enthusiast an interesting picture of (say) a Gresley 'Pacific'. He looks, and registers polite interest. Then he murmurs enviously, 'Wasn't York station fascinating in 1934?'—and I realize with a pang how much more I might have recorded. Forgive me, but in the early days a roll of film was quite an item, at 1 shilling a time. Then, of course, we did not have colour. Come to think of it, during World War 2 we did not even have *film* . . .

Mercifully, all through my well-meaning, if somewhat misguided, apprenticeship there existed a number of totally organized and dedicated men who *did* record the total railway scene. Hebron, Mackay, Ransome-Wallis, Casserley—are among the railway photographic giants and the pleasure they have afforded succeeding generations is almost endless. Certainly, for decades I, and many others, have eagerly collected their work, for it offers a veritable tapestry of railway history. From this background then you will understand the excitement and sheer delight I felt a few years ago when, quite by accident, I acquired—and probably rescued from oblivion—a precious collection of negatives, many of them of railway subjects, by an 'unknown' photographer. His name was Frederick Charles Le Manquais.

Curiously, I never met the man. But possession of his notebooks, carefully compiled over the years 1928–68, persuade me to regard him with greatest respect. He was not only intelligent and enthusiastic, but hugely methodical in his approach. All film 'shots' are carefully numbered, and exposure times are invariably recorded, as, too, are subsequent development details, plus a note of any darkroom 'accidents'! The mere mention of Kodak 120 film in 1928 suggests that he, too, enjoyed the capricious delights of a Kodak Autograph folding camera, and cheerfully joined the rest of us in grappling with slow film speeds which would be totally unacceptable nowadays. Hence, I smile in wan recognition as I read that film No 9, for instance, its contents having been exposed mainly at F4.5 and 1/25th of a second, was 'developed for 27 minutes'. How well I recall the drill! In those days film could be safely developed in naked red light, and once the celluloid was detached from its protective paper wrapping one's immediate objective was to thread it under the raised middle prong of a china 'trident' which lay in the developing dish. Developer, usually home-mixed, was then added; and from there one could anticipate 25 minutes or so of arm-aching 'see-sawing' as images slowly revealed themselves against the yellow coating of the film. Once full development (a matter for personal judgment) was achieved the developer was poured off. After that came more 'see-sawing', this time in a dish full of 'hypo'. Gradually, the yellow coating dissolved, and, welcome sight, a length of clear celluloid was carefully transferred to the kitchen sink for prolonged washing. What a game! But what *excitement*! And then came printing and/or enlarging—another drama in its own right.

But what of Le Manquais himself? What kind of a chap was he? I could make a pretty shrewd guess from the evidence of his notebooks alone, but, fortunately, I have also been able to fall back on the testimony of his sister and his elder daughter. He was born at Merton Park, near Wimbledon, on 17 March 1910, and he died in Welwyn Garden City, after a remarkably active life, on 13 December 1968. His father, a man of Jersey stock, spent *his* boyhood in Swindon and, though never connected with the GWR, he obtained engineering expertise the hard way, by serving in Beyer Peacock's Gorton shops. Later he became a draughtsman and designer. Interestingly, Le Manquais' sister's initial recollection was: 'I do not recall that my father was particularly enthusiastic about railways, thereby influencing my brother in this respect'.

That seemed odd to me, for perusal of his notebooks suggested that young Freddie, as he was known, was fascinated by railways from the word 'go'. Patently, he had the type of mind which relished technical detail. Then his sister followed up with second thoughts, and the jigsaw fell into place:

'On recollection I think my brother was fascinated as a schoolboy by track layouts and signalling systems, more than by actual trains. We lived not far from Clapham Junction, and he could, with care, draw accurate track layouts of that place. His notebooks and scrap paper were filled with drawings of railway lines and signalling systems. Later he joined a model club, and spent all his pocket money on this hobby. Eventually he combined his two hobbies of photography and railways, but he was also very interested in and knowledgeable about canals.'

Then follows valuable insight into the character of the young man:

'Freddie in his younger days was a rather solitary person. He enjoyed long walks, and hardly went anywhere, or on holiday, unless he could go by train. He graduated with a BSc in Physics and Maths at the Royal College of Science around 1932. Later, he qualified as a Chartered Electrical Engineer, and his first job was with Murphy Radio in Welwyn Garden City. He stayed with that firm, which eventually became Ranks, until his death in 1968.'

For my part this simple testimony casts revealing light on why and how Le Manquais got about the way he did. He was, quite simply, a 'loner'. Hardly a week passed without him investigating some railway corner or other, and his notebooks reveal details of astonishingly complex journeys—in England, Scotland, Ireland, on the Continent. His visits to Ireland, in particular, were so convoluted in nature that I assumed automatically that he must have employed a private car—and was suitably abashed when his daughter assured me that her father did not learn to drive until 1948. What a man! It was all done by train and bus. He must, too, have kept himself well informed of current railway developments, for he had an intriguing habit of turning up at the most outlandish places just as another chapter of railway history was about to be closed.

A keen photographer, like his father, Freddie Le Manquais no doubt wielded a camera from boyhood days. For him the crux probably came in August 1928, when he was invited to act as 'chaperon' to two elderly great-aunts who were about to visit Switzerland. Clearly he enjoyed photographing the delightful scenery around Interlaken, but in the process he also contrived to single out some interesting railway subjects, both steam and electric, for attention. As happened to so many of us, the railway photographic 'bug' had bitten. Consequently, the summer of 1929 saw Le Manquais firmly embarked on what was to be a lifelong journey of photographic exploration. The illustrations in this book, all part of his railway output, tell their own story of his progress through the United Kingdom over the following decade. They take us right to the brink of World War 2. On that melancholy occasion, of course, we *all* had to put our cameras away for the duration.

I have not counted the number of Le Manquais negatives in my possession, for many are products of his acute sense of observation where scenery, his country's heritage, and his own family were concerned. But I calculate from his notebooks that during 1929–39 he took some 1,500 photographs. More than half of these were 3¼in × 2¼in in format. Then, as more sophisticated equipment came his way, 2¼in square negatives took over. Typical of his exactitude and method, his 1939 photography finished, rather abruptly, in mid-spool, at exposure No 49.2. Being Le Mauquais, he calmly resumed, five years later, at exposure No 49.3! Having set up home by then in Welwyn Garden City, he was soon blessed with two young daughters—

and, such was his love of family, their upbringing quite monopolized his camera for some time to come.

At last came a time when his family could accompany him on many a trip, home and abroad. Railways again crept into the scheme of things. So, too, did boating holidays. Camera followed camera, as did 35mm film in 1964—both colour and black and white. Rather poignantly, his last 2¼in square negatives, in addition to embracing a final 'shot' of his home on Xmas Day 1967, commemorate an exploratory walk he gallantly undertook over former Cromford & High Peak Railway metals. My guess that his health was failing by now proved to be only too accurate. Within months he was a very sick man.

As it happened, railway subjects feature in his very last 35mm exposures: for his notebooks testify that at 11.45 on the morning of Monday, 28 October 1968, positioned not far from his home by a favourite lineside spot near Digswell, he captured Gresley's masterpiece, No 4472 *Flying Scotsman* as it sped past on an Up special train. Thereafter, silence reigns—and less than two months later the pain he had so bravely borne was finally eased.

What more can one say? I would dearly like to have met Frederick Le Manquais, for despite our vastly different characteristics I recognize him clearly as a kindred spirit. Alas, life being what it is, all I can do is present some of his railway work before you. May I add in conclusion that I am deeply touched by his family's willingness to assist me in assuming this proud privilege?

Theydon Bois,
Essex.
October 1988   T.M.

F.C. Le Manquais
1910–1968

CHAPTER ONE

SOUTHERN RAILWAY

Fortuitously for one who was destined to become both a lifelong railway enthusiast and a Chartered Electrical Engineer, Le Manquais was born in an interesting locality at an interesting time. The Southern Railway may well have been the smallest of the Big Four when it was formed on 1 January 1923, but it by no means lacked charisma, as its various statistics show. A total of 2,281 locomotives, 7,500 coaches, and 36,749 wagons fell to its lot at Grouping. Yet, by the nature of its make up, the SR was the only member of the Big Four whose freight receipts fell short of those earned by handling passengers. Its annual passenger train mileage, in fact, at just under 40 million grossly exceeded freight traffic by a ratio of 6 to 1: though, interestingly, the ratio dropped to 3 to 1 when final translation was made into cash receipts. As they say in the North—'Where there's muck, there's brass . . .'.

Other statistics add piquancy to the SR's stature. The company started life owning 41 steamships and 11 miles of docks and quays. Trackwise the longest tunnel it possessed was one of just under two miles, near Sevenoaks, and a gradient of six miles at 1 in 80 up to Honiton Tunnel posed its most severe major climb. More significantly, however, two major London stations, Victoria and Waterloo, were already involved in the 74 route-miles of electrified track SR inherited and two more, Charing Cross and Cannon Street, were due to be added within the next few years. With the final decision firmly made in 1925 to abandon London Brighton and South Coast Railway's pioneering overhead electrical system, the SR elected thereafter to attach complete faith in the 'third rail' as it strove vigorously to contain rapidly increasing suburban and Home Counties passenger traffic.

This, then, was the ambience to which young Le Manquais was introduced, and with Wimbledon and Clapham Junction, two positive nerve centres, lying nigh it was hardly surprising that Southern Railway operations fascinated him from schoolboy days. Possession of a camera no doubt added immeasurably to his pleasure. Consequently, one fine day in May 1929 he bravely launched out on what was to be an astonishingly peripatetic railway photographic career.

28 May 1929

28 May 1929: Le Manquais' first essay at railway photography in the UK produced this fine study of his home station, Merton Park. Originally called Lower Merton when the Tooting, Merton & Wimbledon line, owned jointly by the London and South Western Railway and the LB&SCR, opened on 1 October 1868, the station was given a third platform in 1870 to accommodate Wimbledon & Croydon line trains. One such, still hauled by a Brighton 'D1' 0–4–2 tank, is seen in this view. As quality housing began to expand locally, the station moved up the social scale, adopting the name Merton Park from 1 September 1887. Passenger receipts, however, suffered a decline after World War 1, as electric tramcars and motor bus services bustled in competition. Then, on 13 September 1925, came a near crippling blow, when the Underground, previously held at bay at Clapham Common, opened its extension through Collier's Wood, and pressed on, deep into the heart of SR territory, to Morden. Fortunately, the SR elected to electrify Wimbledon & Croydon's single line in 1930 and to this day, despite later attempts at closure, BR electric trains, passing each other on occasional double tracks, still serve Merton Park in time-honoured fashion.

27 July 1929: All quiet at Beddington Lane. When the original Wimbledon & Croydon Railway commenced operations on 22 October 1855, its single track passed through a small station known as Beddington. Like many other

27 July 1929

country stations, however, it lay some two miles from the village it purported to serve. Accordingly, it was more accurately restyled Beddington Lane in January 1887. By this time the LB&SCR had acquired W&CR's assets, and were now sole owners of the line. In the long run the absence of housing development in the locality meant that passenger demands between Wimbledon and Croydon remained disappointingly light. Thus, Beddington Lane, with other intermediate stations, gradually declined to the status of an unstaffed halt during World War 1. By 1927 a visit from one daily freight train was quite sufficient to serve its modest private siding. By then, too, the Wimbledon-Croydon section was one of only two parts of SR's suburban system which remained unelectrified. No doubt Le Manquais, in taking this picture, knew what the next year would bring.

10 July 1930: Twelve months duly passed, and the new single line electrified service between Wimbledon and West Croydon had only been in operation four days when this picture was taken of one of its green-painted two-car sets leaving Mitcham station. The three coats of white lead paint which were lavished on each coach roof certainly show to advantage! Conditions attending departure from Mitcham station seem peculiarly cramped but, despite that, SR contrived to maintain a twenty-minute service at peak times and thirty minutes off-peak—seven days a week.

Operated by conductor-guards, these two-car sets had an unusual history, for they were conversions from ex-LB&SCR South London line trailers. Declared redundant in 1911, the trailers, once modified, served for years on main line duties, before SR, installing electric traction equip-

10 July 1930

ment, elected to employ them in pairs on the newly-electrified Wimbledon-Croydon line. The units functioned thus until 1954, when they were obliged to give way to rather smarter BR 2EPB two-car sets.

Another SR development which attracted Le Manquais' attention in the late 1920s was the building of the new Wimbledon & Sutton line. For decades the thriving town of Sutton had been served exclusively by LB&SCR; much to the vexation of the LSWR, who, over the years 1882 and 1891, made innumerable unsuccessful representations to Parliament on the subject. Twenty years later came a stroke of

29 May 1929

luck, when a proposal, hatched jointly by the LSWR and Metropolitan District Line, to construct a 5½-mile link between Wimbledon and Sutton finally captured Parliamentary approval. Unfortunately, capital deficiency and First World War restrictions combined to ensure that little progress was made.

In post-war years, the matter flared up again, when the Underground produced a thrusting new plan to extend its City & South London tube southward to Morden. By now the LSWR's interest had evaporated, but the newly formed SR, duly alarmed at the prospect of losing Sutton and district traffic to the Tube, had no hesitation in expressing its Board's deep concern. Prolonged recriminations followed, and the ensuing dust did not settle until 1924, when a compromise was reached. Under Parliamentary legislation the Tube *was* allowed to extend to Morden—and powers to construct the Wimbledon & Sutton line were duly passed to Southern Railway.

The underground extension to Morden duly opened in 1926. Yet, although SR passenger traffic felt the impact immediately, progress on the new Wimbledon–Sutton line was, for a variety of reasons, lamentably slow. Work at the Wimbledon end did not commence until October 1928, and a further year elapsed ere the main contractor could make a start at Sutton.

29 May 1929: Well aware of current local developments, Le Manquais finished his first roll of film at Wimbledon station by obtaining this view of ex-LB&SCR 'T' Class 0-6-0T No A603 as it arrived on a Wimbledon & Sutton construction train. Rightly described as 'a child of conflict', the new electrified line, now rapidly approaching completion, opened as far as South Merton six weeks later, and its entire 5½-mile length was made available for public service from 5 January 1930. Capital costs were just over £1 million.

Meanwhile, the SR's main London termini did not escape our young man's attention:

4 September 1930

4 September 1930: Less than two years old when this photograph was taken, SR 'Lord Nelson' No E858 *Lord Duncan* made a fine sight at Victoria. The 5,000-gallon Urie tender with turned-out coping appeared on only three 'Nelsons' (Nos E858–860) when the locos were shopped from Eastleigh Works in 1929, and all were later traded in for the more hand-some flat-sided tender. During the summer of 1930 nine 'Lord Nelsons' and a brace of 'King Arthurs' were stationed at Battersea shed to handle SR's Continental link. Their varying success led to subsequent 'Lord Nelson' modifications.

Within a year or two, particularly as advanced educational studies required regular attendance 'in town', Clapham Junction, a great favourite of Le Manquais since boyhood, also began to assume irresistible attractions as a highly desirable locale for lineside photography.

29 March 1933

29 March 1933: A peaceful interlude at Clapham as ex-LSWR Class 'K10' 384, looking quite beautiful in full passenger livery, awaits permission to proceed. Nine Elms built forty of these mixed traffic 4–4–0s for Dugald Drummond in 1901–2, and the LSWR soon found ample use for the 'Grass-hoppers', as they became known. Original intention to shop the 'K10s' with eight-wheeled 4,000-gallon tenders was not implemented; thus the locos emerged with the smaller 3,500-gallon variety, some new, some second-hand. That seen in our photograph came from class 'T9' No 122.

The stovepipe chimney is also something of an anachronism, and is a relic of June 1925, when ten 'K10s' were transferred to Eastern Section to meet a temporary locomotive shortage. Four of them later recovered their taller Drummond chimneys, but No 384 retained her stovepipe to the end. Though withdrawal of the class commenced in January 1947, 31 'K10s' still contrived to enter BR stock. No 384 eventually become the last survivor and just missed completing fifty years service by being scrapped in mid-August 1951. At least it had the consolation of putting in 1¼ million miles.

13 April 1933 (1)

13 April 1933: Southern Railway's new electrified services between London and Brighton commenced running on 1 January 1933, and, typically, ex-LSWR 0-4-4T No 40 takes a back seat at Clapham as the new 'Southern Belle' sweeps through on its fifty-mile dash south. Two of the three five-car Pullman sets initially provided by Metropolitan Cammell have been compounded on this occasion; thus offering accommodation for eighty first class and 312 third class passengers, all, of course, at supplementary fare. The title 'Southern Belle' was changed to 'Brighton Belle' in the mid-summer of 1934.

The Pullman cars, withdrawn in 1942 and placed in store, eventually acquired British Rail livery by 1969, and led a charmed existence until 1972. Even then few were cut up, and most survive in private hands to this day.

13 April 1933: Up to October 1940 quite a brisk passenger service was conducted by the SR between Addison Road, Kensington and Clapham Junction. Journey time was equally brisk at seven minutes. Former LSWR trains, mostly push-pull, used the northern spur at Clapham to enter their own half of the station, while trains following LB&SCR tradition, such as the one seen here with 'D3' 0-4-4T No B398 at its head, burrowed under Clapham's complex network of tracks to emerge on the Brighton side of

13 April 1933 (2)

the station. In post-Second World War years an unsung, and much modified, service—ultimately the last local steam-operated trains in London—catered for workmen only. The three intermediate stations, West Brompton, Chelsea and Battersea, have, of course, long since closed.

Meanwhile, the photographic implications of inter-company traffic at Addison Road, Kensington did not escape our young photographer, and an autumn morning spent there in 1935 proved eminently satisfactory. Relations between the LNWR and LB&SCR were always cordial in pre-Grouping days, and that, plus the ramifications of West London and West London Extension Railways traffic, meant that Addison Road was the veritable eye of a needle through which passed, at some time or other, locomotives from all of the Big Four companies. That, in itself, was a wonderful prospect for any lineside observer.

10 August 1935: For thirty years by this time, with minor interruptions, a regular daily passenger service, known first as the 'Sunny South Special' and later rechristened the 'Sunny South Express', plied between Brighton and Liverpool/Manchester. Metals through Addison Road provided the vital link, and engines were changed at Willesden. In this view the southbound express is being handled by ex-LSWR 'T9' No 313, and in the background ex-LNWR 0–8–0 No 9266 adds additional interest as it awaits its next freight-handling move.

The 'T9', meanwhile, looks different, and is different, from the specimen which presently graces our national locomotive collection. To begin with, it was one of a last batch of fifteen shopped from Nine Elms in 1901,

SOUTHERN RAILWAY

10 August 1935 (1)

a group readily distinguishable by their wider cabs and splashers. Later superheated, as were all 'T9s'—whence the engines really justified their nickname 'Greyhounds'—No 313, in common with nine others, lost its distinctive eight-wheeled 'watercart' tender in 1925, and acquired the one seen here, a smaller six-wheeled one off '700' Class 0–6–0 No 308. The object of this exercise was to enable the 'T9s' to be used on SR's Eastern Section, where turntables were shorter.

10 August 1935 (2)

21

10 August 1935: Kitson products, but clearly GNR in origin, Class 'H1' 4-4-2 No 2041 *Peveril Point* (maker's No 4355/1906) and four sister engines were built as D. E. Marsh's unhesitating response to urgent Brighton demands for fast powerful express locomotives. They, and six 'H2s' added later, duly served their purpose, until they were displaced from Central Section main line duties by the London-Brighton electrification of 1933. Short of scrapping, employment had to be found elsewhere for the 'Atlantics'. Thus, No 2041 emerged from Eastleigh Works in July 1935 with chimney, dome and cab cut down to meet Composite Loading Gauge requirements. One month later Le Manquais photographed it as it passed through Addison Road on an Eastbourne–Leicester train. The leading coach is ex-LNWR.

The following Saturday Le Manquais verified an interesting fact of life, namely that if one knew the ropes, Bricklayers Arms was one of the SR's more 'accessible' sheds. All it required was a little nerve—and records suggest our young enthusiast was never short on that account! Whatever, he took a tram down Old Kent Road, dismounted at the Goods Depot entrance, took a deep breath, and kept on walking. Within a hundred yards came the first signs of locomotive life:

17 August 1935 (1)

17 August 1935: There was nothing about this handsome Class 'L' Wainwright 4-4-0 to suggest German origin, yet No 1779 was, in fact, one of ten such locos delivered by A. Borsig & Co of Berlin to SE&CR in 1914. Built at a time when private UK locomotive manufacturers were too preoccupied to take on fresh orders, Nos 772–781 were landed at Dover right on schedule. German fitters who accompanied them to prepare the locos for service, only just got back to their native land before war was declared. Ironically, the class proved extremely popular with South Eastern men, and played a prominent role in reinforcing wartime railway coastal services. All 22 Class 'Ls' survived well into BR days, and No 31779 was not withdrawn until July 1959. The ex-LB&SCR 'E1' 0–6–0T, No 2164, seen behind in this photograph, bore the name *Spithead* in Stroudley's heyday, and perished, long since nameless, in June 1948.

Following his well-honed instincts, Le Manquais kept going. He was rewarded by this sight a few minutes later.

17 August 1935 (2)

17 August 1935: The locomotive taking water in this delightful study, ex-SECR 'E' Class No 1275, was the second-built of 26 supplied by Ashford Works to H. S. Wainwright's order in 1906–9. Regarded at the time as a usefully powerful expansion of Class 'D' design (the 'Coppernobs' of immortal fame), and later enhanced by superheating, the Class 'Es' served SECR well, and ran enormous mileages during World War 1. Overshadowed later by the success of the Class 'Ls', almost half the class were rebuilt to 'E1' specification by Beyer Peacock in 1920. Nonetheless, all fifteen unrebuilt 'Es', including No 1275, entered British Railways stock in 1948. By then, however, only sporadic employment came their way, and 31275 was withdrawn from Bricklayers Arms in February 1951. In all the locomotive had completed 1,331,508 miles.

The 'School' on the right, patiently awaiting use of the turntable, was No 916 *Whitgift*. Half the forty 'Schools' built eventually acquired

Lemaitre blast pipes and large diameter chimneys. *Whitgift* was one of those which retained its single blast pipe until ultimate withdrawal in December 1922.

At this stage of his life Le Manquais was also displaying an awakening interest in ships, which interest, incidentally, was to flower into small boat ownership in the years after World War 2. Thus, eighteen months later, a Good Friday rail trip to Winchester (see GWR section) was artfully extended to incorporate a brief investigation into Southern Railway activities at Southampton Docks.

26 March 1937

26 March 1937: Resting from their normal dock labours, these ex-LSWR 'B4' 0–4–0Ts were found on shed. *Caen*, seemingly devoid of running number—though it was, in fact, SR No 90—has altered somewhat over the years. One of twenty built for William Adams at Nine Elms in 1891–93, its stove-pipe chimney has given way to one with Drummond-type lip. A tool box has been fitted atop the tank, and a strange object, closely resembling a motorcycle cylinder, is mounted behind the dome. The cylinder, a feature applied to all Dock Department 'B4s' by SR from 1928 onwards, was a linseed filtrator designed to prevent boiler scale. By now, too, green livery has given way to black.

No 93, *St Malo*, seen just inside the shed, offers yet another variation; for it was one of several Southampton Dock 'B4s' whose cabs were cut away fore and aft to improve footplate visibility when shunting. During World War 2, however, cabs were again filled up, and blackout curtains were fitted. *Caen* was withdrawn in May 1948, but *St Malo* held on for another twelve years, and completed 479,705 miles, before bowing to the inevitable in April

1960. Thirteen of the class, which, through additional construction in 1908 reached 25 in number, were sold on to industrial use in post-World War 2 years.

The following month, aware that the former LB&SCR Dyke branch was under threat, Le Manquais returned to the south coast to check the situation for himself.

11 April 1937

11 April 1937: High in the Sussex Downs, ex-LB&SCR 'E4' 0–6–2T No 2505 rests at Dyke station after its sharply curved 3½-mile 1 in 40 climb from Aldrington Halt (formerly Dyke Junction), two miles west of Brighton. Already most passengers have vanished in search of Devil's Dyke, a popular local beauty spot, and presently No 2505 will run round its two-coach train, before resuming a much easier bunker-first descent to sea level, 400ft below.

The Brighton & Dyke Railway, incorporated in 1877, though not opened until 8 September 1887, was always worked by LB&SCR. Nevertheless, it remained independent until it was absorbed by SR in 1923. During the First World War the line was closed, as being of no strategic value, from 1 January 1917 to 26 July 1920. In 1932 Rowan Halt was opened, half a mile up the line, to serve a nearby housing estate, and in the absence of a run-round loop, trains terminating there were, exceptionally, push-pulled. One mile short of Dyke a second halt was opened for the convenience of local golfers. Alas, Dyke branch proved to be particularly vulnerable to bus competition, and, despite tentative employment of SR's Sentinel steam car in 1933–34, the branch was finally closed on 1 January 1939.

By now Le Manquais' photographic activity, railway and otherwise, was growing in both volume and confidence, and countless weekends were spent roaming all over the UK. His energy and curiosity, particularly in railway matters, were boundless, and we happily conclude this chapter with a series of vignettes obtained during 1938–39.

29 January 1938

29 January 1938: As the miscellany of buffer beam hose indicates, ex-SECR 'R1' 0–4–4T No 1710 was on push-pull duty when it was photographed at Westerham. This single line 5-mile branch from Dunton Green was opened by Westerham Valley Railway on 7 July 1881, in response to complaints from local people who had grown tired of journeying five miles to Edenbridge or Sevenoaks to catch a train. Initially, two trains, controlled by electric tablet, were allowed to operate during peak periods. By the late 1920s, however, push-pull trains, with engines supplied by Tonbridge shed, were providing a self-contained service. Then, as 1960 approached, steadily decreasing off-peak traffic clearly put the future of the branch at risk. Although the ultimate posting of closure notices brought vigorous local objections, these were overruled by the Minister of Transport, and the branch closed on 30 October 1961. Hopes that services might be resumed by a preservation society were dashed when work started on construction of the Sevenoaks by-pass.

31 July 1938: When this Sunday morning view was obtained from the Moreton end of Dorchester South station's Down platform SR's locomotive shed was fully operational, and access thereto was gained (left) from behind the platform. Subsequent track alterations by BR, however, meant that engines commenced running straight into the shed from the Down main line. In keeping with this quite unique arrangement points and a ground disc were sited inside the shed building. Thus, as the disc was controlled by the station signal box, Dorchester motive power depot's first road became a mere shunting spur.

31 July 1938

Further changes came on 7 March 1955, when Dorchester shed lost its independent status, though it remained open for the servicing and stabling of locos from other sheds. Then, alas, one shed building was demolished early the following year, and complete closure followed eighteen months later. The final developments came on 22 February 1959, when a new signal box, built on part of the old loco shed site, replaced the lofty ex-LSWR box seen in our picture.

16 October 1938: Sunday morning at Alton station, and SR's auto-train practice is clearly revealed as an Eastleigh train enters behind ex-LSWR 'M7' 0-4-4T No 59. By now the former LB&SCR air control system had gained precedence on the SR, and No 59's reservoir air tank can be seen below the front buffer beam. The variety of hoses are meticulously labelled, for wrong connection to the coaches could spell disaster should an emergency arise. No 59 was, incidentally, the first 'M7' to be painted wartime black. Decades later push-pull working on BR's Southern Region ceased when the last of the 'M7s' were withdrawn in May 1964.

16 October 1938

31 December 1938: Despite the presence of heavy snow a little further north, bright winter sunshine heralded the last day of 1938 at East Grinstead Low Level station as ex-SECR class 'B1' 4–4–0 No 1101 arrived with its train for Brighton. The canopies above the high level platforms which handled Tunbridge Wells-Three Bridges traffic show clearly in the background. East Grinstead's interesting exchange station, the third in a succession of town stations, was made necessary when the line from Lewes became operational in August 1882. Opened some fifteen months

31 December 1938

later, it offered passengers the unusual hospitality of refreshment rooms at both levels. But fortunes change, even for important stations. Once the Lewes line closed in 1958, and subsequent withdrawal of east-west rail services ensured High Level station closure in 1967, East Grinstead's Lower station, rebuilt in its entirety by British Rail, had to be content to assume a more modest role as a branch line terminus.

10 April 1939

10 April 1939: The following spring ex-LB&SCR Class 'H2' 'Atlantic' No 2421 *South Foreland* was observed entering Lewes station at the head of a heavy Up relief Newhaven boat train. The Marsh 'Atlantics' always enjoyed a popular reputation on cross-Channel passenger services and even after electric locomotives took over in May 1949, No 2421 and her sisters continued to appear for a while on Newhaven relief trains over busy periods.

5½ miles long, the section between Newhaven and Lewes was opened in 1847 to develop cross-Channel services to Dieppe. These had previously been maintained from Kingston Harbour, Shoreham. Newhaven Harbour company, later vested in SR in 1926, was created in 1878, and tidal services were replaced by fixed-hour sailings from April 1889.

Brighton-built in June 1911, and named by SR in February 1926, *South*

Foreland served well into BR days before being withdrawn, with a total mileage of 1,112,849, in August 1956.

Our last photograph in this chapter offers both an epilogue and a vivid reminder of the splendour of Southern Railway locomotive power a month or two before World War 2 descended with such devastating long-term consequences for all concerned.

15 July 1939

15 July 1939: Both sporting Bournemouth/Waterloo headcodes, two of Southern Railway's best loved express passenger types pose elegantly at Bournemouth Central. Class 'N15' locos were first introduced by Robert Urie in 1918, but No 784 *Sir Nerovens*, with its Ashford-pattern cab, is clearly recognizable as one of thirty 'King Arthurs' added by NB Loco- motive Company, Glasgow to R. E. L. Maunsell's order in 1925. They were soon nicknamed 'Scotsmen'. Though No 784's original Urie-type 5,000- gallon tender served all through its life, the locomotive itself did not es- cape experiment for during 1947–54 it ran with a (largely unsuccessful) wide spark-arresting chimney. Allocated initially to Bournemouth shed, 784 remained there until early war years but was at Eastleigh when it was withdrawn from service in October 1959.

Companion loco, 'Lord Nelson' No 864 *Sir Martin Frobisher*, looks much more puissant than it did when it was shopped from Eastleigh Works in November 1929. Smoke deflectors apart, the most radical changes in the locomotive's appearance were effected in January 1939, when, after a visit to Eastleigh, No 864 emerged with wide chimney and a smart new ten- der. The latter had interesting origins. At speed the 'hunting' motion of two-cylinder engines such as the 'King Arthurs' kept shuffling coal forward in the tender. Such, however, was not the case with the four-cylinder 'Lord Nelsons', which rode so steadily that firemen were often obliged towards the end of long journeys to expend flagging energies on shovelling coal forward by hand. Bulleid eliminated the problem by introducing self-trimming tenders, whose steeply forward-sloping floors provided the necessary momentum.

Ousted eventually from main line duties by SR's rebuilt 'Pacifics', all sixteen 'Nelsons' were stationed at Eastleigh by October 1959. The first fell foul of the breakers in May 1961, and No 30864, with over 1¼ million miles to its credit, followed suit in January 1962.

CHAPTER TWO

THE 'MET' AND LONDON TRANSPORT

The gaily coloured London Underground pocket map which, year after year, is so eagerly acquired by information-seeking tourists well merits our own close study, for there, coloured part-purple, part-yellow, still lies the very genesis of London Transport. Strange shocks, in fact, await the unwary tourist as he forsakes the claustrophobia of the Central or Northern Line for the Inner Circle, and finds himself in a somewhat faded fairyland of lofty-roofed stations, and walled cuttings which penetrate deep into the heart of the City itself. Did he but know it, this area swarmed with diminutive steam tank engines over a century ago.

Thanks to conflicting pressures from the Great Western and Great Northern Railways the Metropolitan Railway commenced operations between Paddington and Farringdon Street on 10 January 1863 with mixed-gauge tracks. This proved a blessing seven months later, when the GWR, who up to now had been entrusted with operating the Met line, using broad-gauge rolling stock, took umbrage over sundry disputes and declared its intention of withdrawing from the arrangement. The GNR came to the rescue with steam-condensing locos and rolling stock, and, with its middle rail having been thus baptised, Metropolitan Railway management wisely decided to retain both standard and broad-gauge services once the dispute with GWR healed. Unwilling, however, to place themselves again at the mercy of Paddington, they ordered eighteen standard-gauge 4–4–0Ts from Beyer Peacock. In the event broad-gauge operations on the Met finally came to an end on 15 March 1869.

Between the years 1864 and 1884, while the Inner Circle, compounded jointly by the Met and District Railways, was groping its way towards completion, London's stud of Beyer Peacock tanks multiplied remarkably. The Met ultimately acquired 66, and the District Railway, 54 and thus for decades these tiny steam bees buzzed round the Inner Circle—Met locos travelling clockwise, District anti-clockwise—until electrification arrived in 1905 to relieve Londoners from their fumes. The last surviving District tank lived on to 1928. Happily, No 23 of the Metropolitan fleet escaped the breakers, and, duly restored, rests now in London Transport's Museum. Back in the early 1930s it was still active, and could be observed, with sister engines, working on the Met's Brill branch, the one time Wotton Tramway.

Meanwhile, the Met, abandoning Inner Circle inhibitions, was thrusting northwards with its 'Extension Line' from Baker Street. By 1892 its operations reached as far afield as Verney Junction, 50½ miles distant. Powerful electric locomotives were now required to handle booming passenger commuter traffic, and these duly arrived in 1905. British Westinghouse supplied the first ten, and, profiting from experience, the Met ordered ten more from BTH the following year. Then in 1921–23 came the classic Met electric locos when Metropolitan-Vickers were entrusted with the task of nominally 'rebuilding' all previous twenty engines. All evidence suggests, however, that most of the twenty new locos were *built* by Vickers, and were not, in fact, 'reconstructions'.

Le Manquais, patently aware of developments on the Met, chose to investigate for himself in one early visit to London:

13 June 1930

13 June 1930: One could always find a Met electric locomotive 'standing by' at Baker Street station. On this occasion it was No 3 *Sir Ralph Verney*, beautifully liveried in maroon, with the Met crest shining bravely at each end. The advertisement in front of the loco is particularly relevant; for one of the standby loco's duties was to deliver coal for the boiler house at

Chiltern Court. Once the shunt was completed the engine took the empty wagons back to Neasden. Chiltern Court, completed by the Met in 1929, was originally intended to be a hotel, but finished up as a complex of prestigious flats. The need to deliver coal supplies, however, vanished in 1961.

By the end of 1932 the Met, with 99 route miles under its belt, was carrying 110 million passengers a year, and handling over 4 million tons of freight. Yet the end of its independent existence was nigh—for on 1 July 1933 it became part of London Passenger Transport Board. Locomotive side tanks now began bearing the legend 'London Transport'. The Met, of course, never owned a tender engine. In the process of amalgamation LPTB automatically fell heir to the Met's lease of what was known as the 'Brill branch'. The latter was still the property of the Oxford & Aylesbury Tramroad, who had purchased the original Wotton Tramway away back in 1894, and leased it five years later.

In the year 1899 acquisition by the Met of Wotton Tramway, a 6½-mile light railway built in 1871 by the Duke of Buckingham, ostensibly for mineral and agricultural use on his Wotton estate, must have seemed a strange action for a London railway to take. In truth it reflected a very real facet of the Met's burning ambition to thrust outwards from the Metropolis, and gain recognition as a mainline concern. As far back as 1874 the Met's Chairman, Sir Edward William Watkin, had spoken grandly of 'connecting your great terminus (Baker Street) with Northampton and Birmingham and many other important towns . . .' Here, Oxford was the target. Yet, despite businesslike preparations which included rebuilding Quainton Road station and reserving a special platform for Brill branch trains, the Met's gamble, as we shall see, was doomed to failure.

Le Manquais first visited the Brill branch in the summer of 1934. Nothing, he was pleased to note, had changed. He travelled from Quainton Road in the single coach provided—one of the Met's rigid eight-wheeled Oldbury vehicles, *circa* 1865—and he and 4-4-0T No 48 duly arrived at Brill half an hour later. Evidence that photographs that day were taken at F4.5 with a shutter speed of 1/25th second suggests that the weather was none too propitious, and after prowling round Brill station Le Manquais accompanied No 48 on her return journey. A disappointing day, photographically speaking.

By June the following year, in course of a visit to the LNER shed at Neasden, Le Manquais was, however, fortunate enough to capture one of London Transport's lesser steam fry.

8 June 1935: No 102 was one of two 0-6-0STs, of standard industrial design, which were supplied to the Met by Peckett & Sons in 1897–99. Weighing 39 tons, they were used for freight transfer work at Finchley Road and Harrow. Then, as more powerful tanks came on the scene, they gradually drifted towards more parochial work at Neasden Depot. Last of the pair to go, No 102, by then renumbered L54, was withdrawn in 1961.

By now, however, rumours were hardening anent the Brill branch. LPTB, it seemed,

8 June 1935

were preparing to abandon their unprofitable asset. Later that year official pro-nouncement was made that the branch would close on 30 November 1935. Le Manquais set aside one Saturday afternoon to conduct his own investigation.

9 November 1935

9 November 1935: In this view of Quainton Road station, taken looking towards Aylesbury, LPTB's single-tracked Brill branch sweeps in from the right, and one of five rigid eight-wheeled coaches used on the branch lies temporarily out of action. Shortly after this picture was taken 4–4–0T No 23 arrived from Brill, trailing coach No 41. The little tank now bore

'London Transport' on its sides. The coach, unusually, was inscribed 'London Transport—41—Metropolitan'.

His appetite whetted by this arrival, Le Manquais decided to follow the branch on foot. Not far out from Quainton Road he discovered, and photographed, a length of rail bearing an unlikely maker's name: 'Krupp, Essen—1891'. This, of course, was a relic of Oxford & Aylesbury Tramroad track-laying operations immediately after it purchased Wotton Tramway in 1894. Pushing on in hope of further discoveries, Le Manquais then photographed Waddesdon Road station before turning back: he knew he would return. Meanwhile, a sight of 2–6–4T No 115K, still in full Metropolitan Railway regalia, on a freight train at Quainton Road cheered him on his way home.

And back, indeed, Le Manquais came on the occasion of the Branch closure on 30 November 1935. He arrived at Quainton Road in time to identify what was to be the star of the day, 4–4–0T No 41, as it left on the 12.55 pm for Brill. Then he more or less followed the train up the line, using his camera, despite appallingly inclement weather. That day, the last daylight train left Brill at 3.12 pm, again under charge of No 41. The latter, incidentally, no longer carried condensing gear. The train consisted of two coaches, Nos 41 and 45, and Le Manquais' notes suggest an influx of passengers from Oxford University Railway Society may have accounted for this. By now dusk was falling. So, too, was heavy rain and he decided to forego the pleasure of witnessing the midnight celebrations which accompanied the arrival at Quainton Road of Brill Branch's very last train. Rails were severed at the stroke of midnight, and another chapter of railway history was closed.

Or was it? Interestingly, Le Manquais revisited the Brill Branch scene almost three years later, and obtained a splendid series of reminiscent photographs for his pains. One, in particular, involved an unexpected 'find':

4 September 1938 (1)

4 September 1938: Remarkably, a short section of original Wotton Tram-way could still be found, slightly north of Church Siding, in the year 1938. As can be seen, the rails, supplied in 21ft lengths, were of bridge pattern; and the Vignole system of laying them on longitudinal sleepers provided sufficient bearing surface for the 2½ tons per wheel horse-drawn loads originally envisaged. Laid between the longitudinal timbers, tough wooden transomes and wrought-iron tie rods, spaced at 12ft intervals, ensured that gauge was held firm. Rather unexpectedly, track ballast proved, *pro rata*, to be the most expensive item; for it had to be brought from Buckingham by LNWR to Verney Junction, and thence by Aylesbury & Buckingham Railway to Quainton Road.

In 1894 increased axle loading saw the track, now under O&A manage-ment, relaid with 50lb flat-bottomed rail, spiked to conventional trans-verse sleepers. Then, of course, the Met laid heavier rail still in 1910.

4 September 1938 (2)

4 September 1938: In this view, taken looking east from Wotton station's former platform, the old Brill branch trackbed passes under the LNER bridge which carried the (GCR) spur to Grendon Underwood from the Princes Risborough–Birmingham main line. A GWR & GCR joint station was opened at Wotton in 1905; and, so close was it to the Brill branch station, that the two stations shared a joint station master. This is the kind of economy one would more normally associate with Colonel Stephens!

4 September 1938: Five miles out from Quainton Road, and standing by Brill Branch's fourth level crossing, only a mound of earth remains of Wood

4 September 1938 (3)

Siding station's single platform. Its modest length stretched at one time right to the nearest edge of the iron bridge. The latter, since dismantled, carried the Brill branch over the GWR's line from Ashendon Junction to Aynho. The GWR, incidentally, also provided a station known as 'Brill & Ludgershall', but, rather typical of country stations, it was sited some miles from Brill itself.

Long before the Brill fiasco, however, the Met's restless urge to expand had found ample expression elsewhere. Again it was Sir Edward William Watkin who paved the way, this time in his joint capacity as Chairman of both the Met and the Manchester, Sheffield & Lincolnshire Railways. The proposition was simple: the Met could offer access to London, the MS&L egress from London—and resolution of this convenient equation led in 1906 to the formation of the Metropolitan & Great Central Joint Committee. By this time Met steam had pushed out as far as Verney, and electrification had been introduced as far as Harrow-on-the-Hill. From this point on the new Joint Committee assumed responsibility for all lines outside the electrified area. In practice, though, the Committee never owned a single locomotive or passenger coach. All services were provided by the GCR and the Met.

Such vigorous development of the Met's 'Extension Line', as it was known, was bound to demand bigger and better motive power; and Metropolitan response between 1891 and 1925 produced an intriguing range of new steam types—all tank locomotives. Most could be observed some time or other at Rickmansworth during the 1930s, for by that time 'Ricky' had graduated as the Met's new 'focal point':

16 October 1937: Once Met electrification was extended, on 5 January

16 October 1937

1925, from Harrow to Rickmansworth, the latter station assumed new importance as the spot where outward-bound electric trains switched to steam, and, of course, *vice versa*. The changeover, fascinating to watch, and reckoned to be the fastest in the world at three minutes, was to remain with us until steam was phased out in 1960. In this view, electric loco No 1 *John Lyon*, having brought in its train from Baker Street, and been duly relieved by a Met 4–4–4T, has retired to Rickmansworth's South Siding, where, in conjunction with other 'spare' locos, No 4 *Lord Byron* and No 2 *Oliver Cromwell*, it awaits its next southbound duty. Meanwhile, a steam-hauled LNER train, bound for Marylebone, recedes in the distance.

Rickmansworth was reached, on 1 September 1887 and the Met 'Extension Line' was further extended two years later to Chorley Wood and Chalfont & Latimer. Then a strange thing happened—the section of track built from Chalfont onward took the form of a single-tracked branch to Chesham. This economical diversion undoubtedly attracted additional traffic but it did not mean that the Met, temporarily 'strapped' for capital, had any intention of abandoning its ambition to see 'Extension' metals reach Aylesbury. That ambition, in fact, became reality in 1892.

Meanwhile, the citizens of Chesham, a progressive town, expressed their pleasure by gifting the sum of £2,000 to the Met, to ensure that a central site was chosen for the station. The Met duly obliged, and ere long, amidst great enthusiasm, a series of 'long excursions' to such delectable places as Crystal Palace evolved. In the more mundane commuter field a steam-hauled shuttle service to Chalfont made convenient contact with main line trains, the fastest of which reached Baker Street in fifty minutes. All through the Met era Chesham branch trains consisted of ordinary stock, conveniently hauled in 'run-round' fashion. Later, during LPTB's period of management, some erstwhile 'Ashbury' electric stock was converted to 'push-pull' use. But it was all still steam-hauled, for, thanks to the intervention of World War 2, electric traction did not come Chesham's way until 1960.

Clearly the history of the Met's Extension Line, with its constantly changing balance of steam and electric traction, was well known to Le Manquais. Indeed, it seemed to fascinate him: from the time he moved to Welwyn in the early 1930s until his death in 1968 he spent many happy observant hours up and down the line. Chesham station was to prove a particular favourite, and he first took his camera there in 1936:

17 November 1936

17 November 1936: Chesham station, looking very like a GCR establishment in this picture, with its water tower, signal box, and canopied platform, may only have been the terminus at the end of a short branch line, but from the outset the Metropolitan Railway endowed it with generous facilities. The run-round loop in the foreground, for instance, not only afforded access to a three-tracked carriage siding, but carried on, far beyond the station platform, to fan out into an extensive goods yard. In post-World War 2 years a bay was constructed behind the station sign in preparation for electric service, but to this day the fabric of the water tower still remains.

South of Rickmansworth other branches off the Met's 'main line' commanded equal attention. A 2½-mile branch to Watford, opened on 31 October 1925 at a cost of £380,000, employed a triangular junction north of Moor Park, and offered a brisk initial daily service of 140 trains. Half of these were Met, electrically-hauled to Baker

Street. The remainder, LNER, were steamdrawn, and served Marylebone. The steam service was later discontinued, leaving the Met in sole charge.

16 October 1937

16 October 1937: A Baker Street train of Metropolitan 'T' Stock, formerly known as 'MV Compartment Stock', prepares to leave Watford station. New housing has already sprung up in the immediate vicinity. Note, too, the traditional Met red diamond on the station sign.

Further south, and much earlier—as far back as 1904—Harrow-on-the-Hill, a locality whose merits were to feature prominently in the Met's subsequent 'Metroland' campaign, acquired significant new importance when Met metals were pushed southwestward to reach Uxbridge. The lush part of Middlesex this embraced, an area long neglected by both GWR and LNWR, had been challenged frequently enough, but ineffectually, by the Metropolitan District Railway in the past. Now, at last, GWR's Uxbridge monopoly had been broken. Alas, financial stringency prevented the District Railway from following the Met's bold example, and a compromise was achieved by linking up in 1910 with the Met at Rayners Lane, whence running powers over Met metals were accepted to reach the desired target. Later, in 1933, the District route to Uxbridge became part of the Piccadilly Line. Meanwhile, thoroughly conversant with Rayners Lane's new role in London Transport strategy, Le Manquais took his camera there in 1936:

> *7 March 1936*: From 1910 onwards the business of supplying coal to South Harrow Gasworks involved a complicated routine as far as Metropolitan Railway was concerned. Here, for instance, a coal train from Harrow-on-

7 March 1936

the-Hill is approaching Rayners Lane behind 'F' Class 0–6–2T No 91. At Rayners Lane station the locomotive will run round its train. Then it will double back, *via* the Piccadilly Line metals seen on the right of the picture, to South Harrow Gasworks Siding, where, once more, a smart run round will have to be effected, to avoid delay to Piccadilly Line trains. In due course the process will be reversed as No 91 returns with a train of gas coke.

With the Gas Company guaranteeing a minimum 14,000 tons of traffic per year, the Met, and its successors, observed this ritual once or twice each weekday for 44 years until gas production ceased at South Harrow, and Gasworks Sidings finally closed on 4 April 1954. Loco No 91, one of four built for the Met by Yorkshire Engine Co in 1916, perished, as L50, four years later.

When London railways, buses, and tramways were finally amalgamated on 1 July 1933 under the common aegis of London Passenger Transport Board, it soon became apparent that Metropolitan Railway 'main line' aspirations were to be overruled by a unified policy of expansion and electrification *within* Greater London and its immediate environs. Nevertheless, a considerable part of the old Met individuality was to persist longer than might have been expected; for an important works programme announced by LPTB in November 1934 only reached partial completion ere World War 2 erupted.

Midway through this five-year period, however, on 1 November 1937, LPTB, anxious to be unburdened of former Metropolitan steam services, passenger and freight alike, handed over eighteen steam locomotives and 270 goods wagons to the LNER. The locos—four Class 'G' 0–6–4Ts, eight Class 'H' 4–4–4Ts, and six Class 'K' 2–6–4Ts—were reclassified 'M2', 'H2', and 'L2', given LNER running numbers, and simply moved from the LPTB's steam depot at Neasden to that of the LNER across the line. Their duties remained as before. Only, in fact, in 1960, when electrification to Amersham and Chesham became a reality, did former Met 'steam' disappear from its native haunts:

30 April 1938

30 April 1938: Situation still normal at Rickmansworth. Former Met 4–4–4T No 108, now LNER No 6420, has taken over a down train brought in by electric loco No 4 *Lord Byron*, and is now ready to proceed to Aylesbury. The graceful-looking tank was one of eight supplied to the Met by Kerr Stuart & Co, to Charles Jones' design, in 1920–21. Under LNER auspices the whole class was transferred from Neasden to the Nottingham area in December 1941. There, possibly because of the shorter chimneys with which they had been fitted, they were regarded as rather indifferent steamers, and the last of the class vanished in November 1947.

The last branch the Met built before being absorbed by the LPTB in 1933 was one just over four miles long, which linked Stanmore, previously an LNWR monopoly, with Extension Line metals about half a mile north-west of Wembley Park. It, too, was a 'child of conflict'; and three intermediate stations were crammed along its length on the strength of the Met Board's confident prediction that the branch would soon be earning £20,000 a year. They proved to be something of an expensive luxury. As it was, only the government's desire to alleviate growing unemployment, and Parliament's approval of substantial aid under the Developments (Loans Guarantees & Grants) Act of 1929, enabled construction of the branch to begin early in 1931. Public service, employing multiple-unit compartment Met stock duly commenced on 10 December 1932. Rush hours apart, when a few trains ran direct to Baker Street, branch passengers had to change at Wembley Park.

Typically, Le Manquais sampled the branch for himself one Saturday in 1937. At that time trains leaving Wembley Park for Stanmore still had to cross fast tracks to reach the branch; and this situation remained until LT constructed a burrowing junction in 1938. The following year saw further developments. A new 2½-mile Bakerloo tube link between Baker Street and Finchley Road was completed, and as a result Stanmore branch changed over entirely to Bakerloo Line operation from 20 November 1939. The original Met island platform, very similar to that at Watford, remains, slightly too high for Tube stock, at Stanmore to this day.

16 October 1937 (1)

16 October 1937: Meanwhile, Le Manquais was astute enough to record that an extensive six-track siding alongside Stanmore station accommodated a surprising number and variety of grey-painted Met/LPTB goods wagons and vans—even cattle trucks. One tends to forget that during the year 1932 alone the Met handled over 4 million tons of merchandise, minerals, and livestock; a ratio of one ton for each thirty passengers carried. The wagons have long since gone, but in the 1980s the sidings still serve as a stabling point for off-duty Bakerloo stock.

16 October 1937: During its first seven years Stanmore branch off-peak

16 October 1937 (2)

service was partly handled by shuttle car. LT 2569, seen here leaving Wembley Park, was one of two Met motor units which, after accident, were converted in 1910 to double-ended shuttle cars. Initially employed at Uxbridge, Addison Road, and Watford, both found their way to Wembley Park in January 1934. One was scrapped in 1938, but LT 2569, with driving trailer added permanently that year, soldiered on until commencement of the much more convenient Bakerloo service to and from Stanmore one year later justified its removal from the scene. Though never used again for passenger service, the shuttle car was, nonetheless, held in reserve until 1942.

The following year our photographer chose to investigate a rather more abstruse element in Metropolitan Railway history—the East London line, a line whose pedigree dated back to 1865. That was the year when M. I. Brunel's abortive under-Thames pedestrian tunnel, connecting Wapping and Rotherhithe, was taken over by the East London Railway. True to intent, trains began to run between New Cross and Wapping on 7 December 1869. Indeed, on 10 April 1876 extension northward to Shoreditch, and subsequent connection with GER metals, enabled rail service to be established between Liverpool Street and South London. The East London line, now with six intermediate stations, offered double track all the way to New Cross. There, alas, only a single platform was provided. None the less, the LB&SCR earned considerable prestige by running direct trains between Brighton and Liverpool Street for all of eight years up to 1884.

The next major step came with electrification of the East London line from 31 March 1913. The Met even contrived to assume its management in 1921, though the Southern Railway acquired ELR's freehold four years later and held on to it, even after LPTB came into being in 1933. Later service between Whitechapel and Shoreditch reverted to a mere shuttle, and four-car sets of vintage District Line stock, with hand-operated doors, were considered adequate for the task. That was the position when Le Manquais, and camera, arrived on the scene one Saturday afternoon:

22 January 1938

22 January 1938: A gloomy picture, but one full of historic interest, as a four-car shuttle leaves East London Line's Shoreditch station for Whitechapel. The platform opposite, unemployed then, has long since been demolished. Both tracks passed on behind the camera to connect with GER/ LNER metals which led to and from Liverpool Street. After nationalization in 1948 complete ownership of the ELR passed to British Rail. Unfortunately, despite the junction's undoubted utility during World War 2, BR soon saw fit to sever the connection, and a single buffer end now exists where LB&SCR engines used to wend their way to foreign parts. From the Shoreditch passenger point of view slightly more modern District Line stock took over until January 1974, when it was replaced by 1938-vintage Tube stock.

Later that month the next station along the line had something a little out of the ordinary to offer. We are now 'upstairs', as it were; for Whitechapel handled East London and District Line traffic operations at different levels:

30 October 1938: Sunday morning on the District line, and LPTB 0-4-4T No L47 provides a welcome diversion as it enters Whitechapel station on a

30 October 1938

short track maintenance train. Known as 'E' Class, the first three of these
sturdy ex-Metropolitan Railway tanks were built at Neasden in 1896–98,
and four more, including No 80, now L47, followed from Hawthorn Leslie
in 1900–01. Although the third-built Neasden loco was numbered 1, the remainder of the class were given Nos 77 to 82. A subsequent gap to 90 in
Met running numbers suggests the company might well have introduced a
further seven 'E' Class tanks, had not electrification intervened. One of four
which survived to enter LPTB stock in 1933, No L47, repaid the compli-
ment by serving another eight years before being withdrawn.

So far no mention has been made of other major arteries in London Transport's railway network. There is, however, ample evidence to show that Le Manquais was
thoroughly alert to developments in all LT areas. Our concluding pictures offer
some indication of the interest he could extract from what was, I fear, to many of us
a fairly drab conventional scene.

18 February 1939: The LPTB fell heir to two stations called Wood Lane.
Both were opened in May 1908, and both were renamed White City in
November 1947. One, originally called Wood Lane (Exhibition), was
opened on the Hammersmith & City (Met) Line with a view to serving the
White City Exhibition. Wooden in construction, it was badly damaged by
fire in October 1959, and never reopened.
    The second Wood Lane station lay on the Central Line, and was in-
tended as a terminal station on a loop which had also been built to serve the
White City Exhibition. Further Central Line extension to Ealing Broadway
in 1920 necessitated provision of two additional single platforms. Thus, an

18 February 1939 (1)

awkward triangular layout evolved, and, with Central London Railway works and generating station both sited hard by, the task of taking trains out of service at night began to occasion progressively complicated running arrangements. By 1927, when crowds attending White City Stadium for greyhound and cycle race meetings reached a new peak, provision of the sharpest curve on the Underground, one of 250ft radius, became necessary. Wood Lane's platform, having also been lengthened on the inner side by 35ft, simply had to be provided with the movable wooden end seen in our picture, to allow trains to enter the depot.

18 February 1939: Here we are looking west from North Acton, not far short of Ealing Broadway, the station which played host to the last extension of Central Line services before LPTB assumed command in 1933. Originally to be called Victoria Road, North Acton was one of two stations added in November 1933 as housing in the district developed.

The GWR was far from averse to Central Line's thrust westward, being quite happy to see its Ealing station benefit from direct Tube service to the City and West End. In fact, it positively relished the prospect, held out at one time, of Central Line metals pushing out as far as Denham. Thus it was the GWR that sponsored construction in the 1930s of a double-tracked line, for exclusive use of the Central Line, between North Acton and Greenford—and possibly beyond. Appreciating, too, that one pair of tracks between Shepherds Bush and North Acton could hardly cope with Central Line traffic to both Ealing and Greenford, as well as GWR steam trains to and from the West London Railway, the GWR obligingly quadrupled the section westward from Wood Lane, and on through North Acton. Accord-

18 February 1939 (2)

ingly, GWR trains ceased to use the electrified lines from 19 June 1938. Ironically, thanks to the intervention of World War 2, Central Line trains did not, in fact, reach Greenford until June 1947.

In this view we have the Central Line on the left, the new GWR West London metals in the centre, and the GWR/GCR main line on the right. An auto-train is about to halt at GWR's platform (now demolished), and the photograph was taken from the footbridge which once connected the two stations.

CHAPTER THREE

LONDON, MIDLAND & SCOTTISH RAILWAY

In the year 1923 any reasonably percipient adult railway observer must have marvelled, and rather expected fireworks, when those responsible for Grouping elected to place both the London & North Western and Midland Railways under common LMSR aegis. Not only were the two companies long established and fierce competitors for north-south traffic, but their individual philosophies were poles apart. Jet black LNWR engines, their drivers unimpressed by loading restrictions, had long been accustomed to roaring north, sometimes hauling outrageously heavy trains, and invariably raising hellfire on the way. Crewe men, proud of the 'Premier Line's' reputation for getting there at all costs, liked it that way.

Alas, the contrast with Midland Railway operating practice could not have been greater; for on that august, and justly famed, 2,000-route-mile network beautifully groomed crimson passenger locos—nothing larger than a 4-4-0—handled carefully calculated loads, and any train which dared to exceed 230 tons automatically attracted a pilot engine. Small wonder was it that Crewe men were deeply aggrieved for, over the first decade of LMSR's existence, Midland practice, and Midland men, emerged as dominant factors in shaping LMSR destinies!

In recent years various railway authors have taken pains to unravel the tangle of personalities, and the regrettable dearth of senior LNWR candidates for high office, which bedevilled the LMSR's first ten years of existence. Logical though the story is, it cannot be denied that the ruthless imposition of MR practice on the whole LMSR network makes painful reading—even in retrospect. At the time, however, youthful lineside observers such as Le Manquais and myself remained blissfully ignorant of such grave implications and were content to hail each new LMSR locomotive type gleefully as it emerged—regardless of whether it was built at Derby or Crewe. Such was the euphoria of the 'Big Four'!

Certainly, where Le Manquais was concerned, the continued operational presence of London's two great LMS termini, Euston and St Pancras, each trying hard to retain its individual characteristics, rather cloaked the immediate, and constant, infiltration of newly built MR-type locomotives. A visit to St Pancras in July 1930, for instance, revealed little other than a sight of 4–4–0 Compound No 1093 leaving at the head of a northbound express. The fact that the engine was built at Derby in 1925 hardly seemed to matter—at the time. Moving on to lusher pastures at Euston in March 1931, the presence of ex-LNWR 4–4–2T No 6782 on local suburban service, plus adjacent attendance by a brace of Crewe-built 0–6–0 saddle tanks on station pilot duties, seemed reassuring enough to any LNWR loco admirer. And yet —what the dickens was MR/LMSR Compound No 1110 (Derby/1925) doing, pulling out of *Euston* on an express train to *Rugby*?

Earlier camera sorties by Le Manquais over a wider London context had tended rather to disarm suspicion:

28 June 1929

28 June 1929: Willesden Junction offers a truly vintage LNWR scene as 0–8–0 No 8986, formerly LNWR No 2535 and Crewe-built in 1895, drifts through on a short goods train. Even the name *Clay Cross* on the leading coal wagon awakens memories of the past! The engine, LNWR Class 'A', was one of 111 three-cylinder compounds built to F. W. Webb's design over the years 1895–99. George Whale, Webb's successor, rebuilt the lot between 1905 and 1912 as two-cylinder 'simples', with smaller boiler. Classified variously as 'C', 'C1' and 'D', they were easily eclipsed, however, by later, more powerful, LNWR 0–8–0s; and the last of the 'C1s', rated only '3F' by the LMSR, vanished in 1933. No 8986, rebuilt to Class 'C1' in May 1910, was withdrawn in December 1930.

11 July 1930

11 July 1930: The spectacle of an ex-Midland Railway locomotive trailing a train of empty coal wagons through Kensington High Street station must have puzzled many who witnessed it. But Class '3F' 0–6–0T No 1922 was, in fact, exercising a long-established right, for MR owned a coal depot nearby, and, in light of its healthy coal traffic between Toton and Brent, was well positioned to maintain supplies. The main difficulty lay in the circuitous route the Midland, and later the LMSR, had to employ to get the coal from Cricklewood to Kensington. This involved intricate use of 'foreign' lines, and consequent tolls which had to paid to LNWR, NLR, LSWR—even the Metropolitan District Line—must have added somewhat to the price of coal at the receiving end. In addition, intense all-day traffic on the District Line ordained that MR coal traffic had to be conducted at night. Presumably, in the circumstances, the '3F' stayed overnight at Kensington.

Less than a year later, though, came interesting indications of the LMSR management's desire, however Derby-orientated it was, to rethink the matter of MR section coal traffic:

17 April 1931: Had this picture been taken five years earlier two ex-Midland 0–6–0s would have been heading north through Hendon with their long train of empty coal wagons, instead of LMS 'Garratt' No 4984. In an attempt, in fact, to eliminate double-heading on Toton-Brent coal trains the LMS ordered three of these 2–6–6–2 monsters from Beyer Peacock & Co in 1927. Four-cylindered, and fitted with 5ft 3in driving wheels, the 'Garratts', it was found, could, despite deficiencies in the detail of their MR design,

17 April 1931

handle 1,500-ton coal trains with ease. In addition they saved not only one set of enginemen, but 15–20 per cent in fuel. Return trains of up to 100 empty wagons were often run at an average speed of 25 mph.

Thirty more 'Garratts', including No 4984, were delivered by Beyer Peacock in 1930. They carried taller chimneys and domes, and tanks and bunkers were larger. Later in the 1930s most were equipped with rotating steam-operated self-trimming bunkers, which luxury increased their working weight to 155½ tons. Later still, BR's ubiquitous Class '9F' 2–10–0s arrived on the scene, and the 'Garratts' were progressively withdrawn in 1955–57. On at least one occasion, however, No 4984 had its own brief moment of glory; when, fitted with temporary vacuum brake, it took part in LMSR passenger train trials. These were not particularly successful, and 4984, renumbered 7984 in 1938 to make way for further instalments of Stanier 'Black Fives', eventually perished in February 1956.

It was strange, but as new LMSR locomotive construction blossomed vigorously into the 1930s it really should have dawned on youngsters like myself that Derby was playing an odd sort of game. Granted, we had no knowledge of the inner workings of LMSR management, but the fact remains that details of newly-built locomotives were freely advertised in such railway press as we read. In any case, stockbooks, with their engaging statistics, later became available. Statistics, however, can be interpreted in many ways—and our trouble was that those we perused stopped short of dwelling on the real significance behind the first ten years of LMSR locomotive building policy.

Consider, for instance, the table printed overleaf. Columns A and B offer the commonly accepted facts. The bald figure, however, in Column B of 2,164 new locomotives constructed by LMSR up to 31 December 1932 warrants much closer examination for no fewer than 1,292 of these were of *already established* Midland Railway design. Nowadays, we know why. Somewhat inconclusive locomotive trials persuaded LMSR management to build 195 more MR 4-4-0 Compounds between 1925 and 1927, and a similar misunderstanding of the value of six-coupled locomotives led to the construction at Derby Works, commencing in 1928, of 98 Class '2P' Midland inside-cylindered 4-4-0s. Responsibility for building forty more was tossed Crewe's way in 1931-32.

On the freight and shunting fronts much the same myopic policy was pursued. 530 MR standard Class '4' 0-6-0s were turned out, by various makers, between 1924 and 1928, and by 1931, 415 new MR Class '3' 0-6-0Ts also found their way into LMSR service. Add some 150 engines of other constituent company design eg, LNWR, L&YR, CR, LT&SR/MR (mostly orders which had been placed prior to

LMSR STEAM LOCOMOTIVE STOCK

Constituent Company etc.	(A) Locos acquired by LMSR at Grouping – 1923	(B) Steam Loco stock as at 31/12/1932	(C) Steam Loco stock as at 31/12/1932 – ADJUSTED
ENGLAND			
LNWR) Amalgamated	3,360	2,021	2,052
L&YR) 1/1/1922	1,654	1,224	1,275
TOTAL LNWR –	5,014	3,245	3,327
Midland Rly	2,925	1,752	3,079
North Staffs Rly	192	88	88
Furness Rly	136	31	31
Miscellaneous Coys	67	–	–
Somerset & Dorset JR (78 locos taken into LMS stock – 1/1/1930)	–	48	48
SUB-TOTALS –	8,334	5,164	6,573
SCOTLAND			
Caledonian Rly	1,077	940	970
Glw & SW Rly	528	109	109
Highland Rly	173	110	110
SUB-TOTALS –	1,778	1,159	1,189
ADD:			
New locomotive construction by LMSR.	–	2,164	725
GRAND TOTALS –	10,112	8,487	8,487

Grouping) and a final realistic total of 725 *new* LMSR locomotives emerges. 705 of these were six or eight-coupled (540 tender, 165 tank), and twenty were Sentinel locos (five shunters, fifteen railcars). In the Table I have adjusted Column B by placing 'like with like'—and Column C is the result. The real eye-opener is that, notwithstanding an extensive scrapping programme over the previous ten years, the LMSR entered 1933 with *more* Midland-design engines than it acquired in 1923!

All through the 1930s, particularly as he completed his studies at the Royal College of Science, Le Manquais kept a watchful eye on LMSR London territory and six photographs which follow offer appropriate comment on contemporary locomotive development. Inevitably, they also evoke memories of events which took place a decade earlier; events which ultimately shook the LMSR Locomotive Committee to its very foundations.

The story starts with the 1924 British Empire Exhibition at Wembley, where the Great Western, not content with displaying *Caerphilly Castle*, proudly publicized it as 'Britain's most powerful express passenger locomotive'. The LNER, whose 'Flying Scotsman' stood adjacent to it, cheerfully threw its hat in the ring by claiming that *its* mighty 'Pacific' was 'Britain's largest express locomotive'. Obliged, perforce, to adopt a less provocative stance, the LMSR made do with exhibiting No 964, a new, and specially built, specimen of the LNWR 'Prince of Wales' genre. Still inside-cylindered, the loco was fitted with Walschaerts valve motion *outside* the frames. Rather a feeble *riposte*, one would have thought, from the mightiest railway company in the land!

The upshot of it all need not be rehearsed here—for it is well and truly enshrined in British railway history. Suffice it to say that only the LNER and the SR were bold enough to pick up the GWR's gauntlet. Conversely, the LMSR, left on the starting line, as it were, found itself in real difficulty in 1926, when its Executive, throwing off much of its Midland inhibitions, resolved to introduce a full blooded (LNWR style) West Coast express passenger service with effect from the summer of 1927. Plans were laid; heavy trains were visualized.

Alas, such loads were patently beyond the powers of LNWR four-cylinder 'Claughtons', no matter how fine their record was. What, then, was to haul these new trains? Common knowledge that both Derby and Horwich were toying with more powerful express locomotive designs afforded little comfort to those concerned; for that implacable 1927 deadline left no room for further experiment. There was only one answer. A drastic solution would have to be found—straight away!

Thus, thanks in the main to Southern Railways's courtesy in releasing 'Lord Nelson' drawings, and heroic co-operation from the North British Locomotive Company of Glasgow, the 'Royal Scots' made their debut in the summer of 1927. Faults they may have had, but the sheer beauty of these new three-cylinder 4-6-0s caused a sensation at the time. LMSR morale soared accordingly.

5 August 1932: However grand Hardwick's great Doric Arch may have looked—and it *was* impressive—the train sheds beyond at Euston were little short of an undistinguished sprawl. The departure side of the station, in particular, was no photographer's paradise; and any enthusiast intent on pointing

5 August 1932

his camera at Main Line departures had but short stretches of wooden-planked platform on which to operate. Hence the claustrophobic, albeit arresting, nature of this study of No 6127 *Novelty* as she prepares to head north with a heavily laden 'Royal Scot'. A pilot has been added, but the loco concerned, a Midland Compound, lies far beyond reach. Fitted with smoke deflectors, as were all 'Royal Scot' locos after a serious accident in 1931, No 6127 still carries the standard MR 3,500-gallon tender with which all fifty of the class were initially, and hurriedly, fitted. The fact that the tender was 18½ inches narrower than the engine could hardly have cheered the train crew's backward view! Later, under Stanier auspices, the 'Royal Scots' were given larger curved-top tenders, and later still, in 1936, *Novelty* was renamed *The Old Contemptibles* in keeping with current LMSR naming policy.

Novelty's massive maroon-clad bulk, meanwhile, has attracted a small knot of spectators. The lady seems particularly intrigued by the loco's name—and we can only trust her companions were able to offer a satisfactory explanation of the etched brass plaque which shone below the name plate itself! The wooden platform on which they stand disappeared, mercifully, by the spring of 1936, when 145ft and 120ft extensions to Departure Platforms 12 and 13 were completed. From thereon, trains of sixteen coaches, exclusive of locomotive, could be comfortably contained; and all at Euston must have breathed a sigh of relief.

1932 was also the year in which W. A. Stanier arrived at Derby to take over the CME reins from Sir Henry Fowler. His avowed intention, that of restoring LMSR locomotive fortunes, was given full support; and, right from the word 'go', the succession of fine modern locomotives he produced embodied the best in GWR and LMSR practice. His first (1933) design, a 2-6-0, aroused interest enough; but when he followed, months later, by shopping two massive 'Pacifics' the railway world really sat up and took notice. Closely modelled on Swindon's *Great Bear*, though clearly possessing the power and ubiquity of the 'Kings'—yet essentially LMSR locomotives—the two 'Princess Royals' soon became something of a showpiece at Euston. Needless to say, Le Manquais did not deny himself a ringside seat.

5 May 1934

5 May 1934: No 6200 *The Princess Royal* makes an impressive sight as she draws into Euston's No 2 Platform with the Up 'Royal Scot'—right on schedule. The inordinate length of the engine quite dwarfs the 4,000-gallon, 9-ton, straight-sided tender with which it was initially equipped. A year later, however, a curved-top tender, holding an additional ton of coal, was substituted, and the loco's proportions were considerably improved as a result. Note, too, the white Caledonian Railway route indicator placed high on No 6200's smokebox. This, if you please, was tacit evidence of Caley men's determination to resist complete domination by Derby. When *The Princess Royal* left Polmadie shed that morning the indicator was placed in position, as clear evidence that she was about to head a southbound express over *Caley* metals. But, when train crews were changed at Kingmoor, and the CR men returned home, patently no one had the heart to remove their beloved symbol. Thus, long after the Scottish railway ceased to exist, Euston was introduced to one of its hallowed practices!

12 May 1934

12 May 1934: It is late afternoon at Euston, in more ways than one; and the setting sun merely emphasizes the sadness of the current LNWR locomotive situation, as 'Prince of Wales' No 5655 *Smeaton* approaches a waiting mail van. Wherever she is bound, the stopping passenger headlamp on her smokebox suggests it cannot be far away. Yet, little more than a decade earier, *Smeaton* was a proud London & North Western express engine, one, of course, of many which thrust their way out of Euston and blazed fiery trails north at the head of important trains.

So far only ten of the 245 'Princes' inherited by LMSR at Grouping have been scrapped. But the next three years will witness such wholesale demolition of the class that only will four live on to enter BR stock in 1948, and these, too, perished within eighteen months. *Smeaton*, a much earlier victim, was withdrawn seven months after the above photograph was taken. Meanwhile, adding salt to LNWR's wounds, and just visible on the left, an MR-type 0–6–0T, one of the famous post-Grouping 'Jinties', settles in to its new role as Euston Station pilot. As yet, LNWR's old station still retains its traditional rambling character.

10 August 1935 (1)

10 August 1935: Despite a steady influx of Stanier locomotives, four engines, casually gathered at the southern end of Camden shed, combine to offer an almost uncanny display of early LMSR locomotive construction. No 1150 was one of 195 Midland Compounds added from 1924 onwards. Her immediate companion, No 2852, originally numbered 13152, a Horwich-inspired Mogul, was reproduced 245-fold. Tucked in behind, the 'Jinty' was one of 415 added to an original MR class by the LMSR, while, just squeezing into the picture, No 6144 *The Honourable Artillery Company* (originally named *Ostrich*) represented the 'Royal Scot' Class of seventy locomotives built by LMSR during the years 1927 and 1930. Seen in that light, this modest Camden assembly was really 'standing in' for a total of 925 LMSR engines!

On 18 March 1933, rather oddly on the face of it, Le Manquais chose to spend his Saturday afternoon by the lineside near Luton. It soon transpired, however, he knew what he was about; for, after witnessing a Midland compound, MR 4–4–0 No 767, and LMSR 'Garratt' No 4992 going about their various duties, he duly captured No 2198, a former London, Tilbury & Southend Railway 4–6–4T as it passed by on an Up local. Delivered direct in 1912 to Midland Railway, after the latter had absorbed the smaller railway, these massive outside-cylindered tanks were a positive embarrassment where Derby was concerned, and energetic, but unavailing efforts were made to effect their sale. No 2198, the last survivor of eight, was eventually withdrawn by LMSR in May 1934, eighteen months before Le Manquais ventured to visit former LT&SR territory—at Plaistow shed, near West Ham. He soon discovered that LT&SR-type 4-4-2 tanks, the famous 'Tilbury Universal Machines', were still perfectly capable of handling Fenchurch Street's intensive suburban traffic.

10 August 1935 (2)

10 August 1935: Coded 13A in the LMSR hierarchy, Plaistow shed was always busiest before and after 'rush hours' on the Tilbury line. Here, after completing their morning stint, a representative line of tank locos queue up for re-coaling. In the foreground is 4-4-2T No 2115, one of ten traditional LT&SR tanks ordered by the MR, and delivered by Derby in 1923. Next comes No 2504, one of 37 Stanier three-cylinder 2-6-4Ts built at Derby in 1934. Possessed of admirable acceleration, these locos served the LT&SR Section well. No 2522, the 2-6-4T last in line, has the same pedigree.

The 4-4-2T third from the camera has a different story to tell. Numbered then as LMSR 2148, it is now preserved in full LT&SR livery as No 80 *Thundersley*. Built as *Southend-on-Sea* by Robert Stephenson & Co in 1909, the loco was renamed *Thundersley* the following year, and after spending a very active life on LT&SR/LMSR/BR service it was finally withdrawn in June 1956. All three major LT&SR sheds, Plaistow, Tilbury, and Shoeburyness, followed suit, by closing to steam six years later.

21 December 1935: Back at Euston Station after a lengthy absence for repairs, No 6202, W. A. Stanier's famous 'Turbomotive' 'Pacific', is again ready to leave for Liverpool (Lime Street). This remarkable locomotive, whose creation was inspired by a visit Stanier made to Sweden in 1932 to investigate the merits of steam turbine working, was built at Crewe Works in 1935. Metropolitan-Vickers Co Ltd of Manchester manufactured and fitted

21 December 1935

the non-condensing turbine. Despite teething troubles with the reverse turbine and lubrication, No 6202, originally projected as a third 'Princess Royal'
loco, effectively proved the worth of high-speed geared turbines on main
line operation. Note the absence of cylinders and valve gear, rendered
unnecessary by the unique drive system. It was mainly employed working
between London and Liverpool: indeed, in post-war years it successfully
handled loads of up to 500 tons, a very desirable objective where LMSR
were concerned. Unfortunately, increasing difficulty in obtaining turbine
spares led, in 1948, to the experimental locomotive being rebuilt, again at
Crewe, in conventional 'Princess Royal' form. Now named *Princess Anne*, the
engine experienced even greater calamity in 1952, when it had to be written
off after involvement in the Harrow railway disaster of 8 October.

By now Le Manquais' travel ambitions were ever widening, and few weekends
elapsed when he did not undertake some interesting journey or other:

27 July 1935: Beautifully liveried in maroon, 'Royal Scot' No 6152 *The
King's Dragoon Guardsman*, one of twenty built at Derby in 1930, cuts a dashing figure as it sweeps southward near Lancaster. The leading coach is
GWR. Yet, all is not as it seems; for in 1933 loco No 6152 exchanged identity with 6100 for the purpose of touring USA and Canada. During the tour
No 6100 was inspected by 3,021,861 citizens, which fact was recorded on a
special nameplate the locomotive bore thereafter. Both loco and plate can be
seen today at Bressingham Steam Museum in East Anglia. The interesting
thing, though, is that the LMSR's deception of 1933 was never rectified—

27 July 1935

therefore the engine in our picture was, in fact, the original *Royal Scot*. In keeping with all others of the class, it was rebuilt with Stanier taper boiler and double chimney in 1945, and, revitalized thus, it served the LMSR and BR faithfully for another twenty years.

The following year Le Manquais had occasion to change trains at Birmingham. Out, of course, came his camera:

4 July 1936: Partly because LNWR never dwelt on ceremony, partly due to the awkward railway approach thereto, Birmingham's New Street station, opened in 1854, was always functional, rather than decorative. Nevertheless, its trussed arch roof held the record for the world's widest span (211 ft) for fourteen years—until Lime Street advanced matters by one foot! Traffic, however, soon became so burdensome that the LNWR built a second station alongside. Separated, oddly, by Queens Drive, the new station, opened in 1885, soon became known as the 'Midland Side'. In this view of the LNWR's original station we are looking north. The footbridge which straddles the platforms also served as a public highway, thus New Street was traditionally an 'open' station. Below the clock in the centre of the footbridge can be seen No 3 signal box, a draughty, smoke-ridden hut which controlled points and signals on the through line between Platforms 1 and 2. The sole locomotive visible is No 143, one of 139 very useful Class '3MT' 2–6–2Ts subscribed by Stanier during 1935–38.

During World War 2 enemy air raids extensively damaged both roofs at New Street, and the LMSR were obliged to demolish that on the LNWR

4 July 1936

side. Replacement, completed in 1948, was makeshift, in view of impending Nationalization; though, fortunately for all concerned, No 3 signal box disappeared in the process. Then, in 1964, all was swept away, and BR created an entirely modern structure, with twelve through platforms.

6 June 1936

6 June 1936: Pausing at York, *en route* to Scotland, Le Manquais chose to capture ex-MR 4-4-0 No 546, Derby-built in 1913, if only as a reminder that the LMSR, too, enjoyed a presence in the NER's great station. Dating back to the halcyon days, L&YR's Liverpool and Manchester trains and MR West of England services all utilized running powers into York. The old Midland circular roundhouse, seen in the background (right), was opened around 1879, and served in various forms, latterly for the storage of surplus locos until it was demolished in 1963. The L&YR's shed, known as Queen Street, lay off left. Its complement of locomotives shrank so low that the MR engines were brought across in 1932, as a measure of rationalization. The expedient proved shortlived, however, and in 1939 Queen Street shed was finally closed.

Some of Le Manquais' wanderings were so convoluted by now that one could spend hours wondering how on earth he employed public transport—rail, ship, and bus—in executing them. Certainly, two important elements—an intimate knowledge of railway timetables and a stout heart—were basic factors in his strategy. One particular week in May 1937 springs readily to mind. On Wednesday, the 19th of that month, he photographed Wareham station; then the lineside by Corfe Castle. The following Sunday was spent on the westernmost part of the Isle of Wight, where The Needles and Alum Bay occupied his attention. Presumably he did not allow himself time to investigate Isle of Wight railways. One must assume, in fact, he returned to London that evening—for by noon next day he was deep in Stratford-upon-Avon & Midland Junction country! What a man! He had been there the year before, exploring Broom Junction, Stratford, and Byfield stations. Now Towcester and Blisworth were his targets.

The S&MJR became part of the LMSR in January 1923. But, of course, it had a venerable history of its own, dating back to 23 June 1864, when construction of a very ambitious East & West Junction Railway was authorized. Both GWR and MR played crucial roles as events unfolded themselves in this controversial area, and once completion of Great Central's main line from London to Rugby in 1899 offered connection with E&WJR trains at Woodford & Hinton the time soon fell ripe for amalgamation between the E&WJR and Stratford-upon-Avon, Towcester & Midland Junction Railway. An Act of 1908 paved the way, and the S&MJR was formed on 1 January 1909. Towcester acquired further links with the outside world when the S&MJR followed up in 1910 by absorbing the Northampton & Banbury Junction Railway.

17 May 1937: 1910 was also the year when this elegant signalbox was provided at the Blisworth end of Towcester station's Down platform. The view was obtained from a replacement footbridge erected by the LMSR in 1926, and, sandwiched between four coaches, ex-LNWR 2-4-2T No 6166 has been caught in the act of leaving with a motor-train for Blisworth. Once past the signals, No 6166 will fork left on the single line to Blisworth. The metals going off right will pass through Stoke Bruern before contacting MR's old Bedford-Northampton line at Ravenstone Wood Junction. Ten

17 May 1937

years later postwar events began to play havoc with the Stratford-upon-Avon section, and, after sundry closures and passenger traffic withdrawals, the last trace of SMJ traffic disappeared in July 1965.

No 6166 fared reasonably well: one of a large batch of 2–4–2Ts shopped from Crewe between 1890 and 1897, it was motor-fitted in 1931. Inadvertently renumbered 26616 by LMSR in 1945, it finally entered BR stock as 46616, and succeeded in outliving its confreres by lasting until September 1955.

The summer of 1937 was about the time, too, when LMSR chose to experiment with a new style of *sans serif* lettering and block numerals on quite a number of their express passenger locomotives. Results, however, were not judged an aesthetic success, and for the remainder of its independent life the LMS reverted to the much more handsome serif type.

29 May 1937: Seen at Willesden, 'Patriot' No 5532 *Illustrious* demonstrates the new LMS style of block lettering. These handsome Class '5X' 4–6–0s were probably the liveliest, and most economical, express engines produced by the LMSR before the advent of W. A. Stanier. The first two, built at Derby in 1930, incorporated parts of former LNWR 'Claughtons'. The next forty, shopped by both Derby and Crewe in 1932–33, were deemed, for accounting purposes, to be nominal three-cylinder 'conversions' of a like number of 'Claughtons'. The last ten, added by Crewe in 1934, were entirely new engines.

Not all of the original 'Claughtons' bore names. No 150, for instance,

29 May 1937

nameless when it left Crewe Works in March 1921, carried *Holland Hibbert* plates temporarily—but only for the purpose of working a Royal Train on 8 October that year. LMSR bestowed the name *Illustrious* upon her in May 1923. Ten years later came withdrawal of the 'Claughton', and the name passed to her 'nominal' replacement. The latter, one of eighteen 'Patriots' ultimately rebuilt with taper boiler and double chimney, lasted until 1964.

The following month our traveller enjoyed a hectic railway fortnight in Northern Ireland. Despite his undoubted exertions, he was still able to demonstrate, on the way home, that his opportunist touch had not deserted him:

27 June 1937 (1)

27 June 1937 (2)

27 June 1937: Both locomotive crew and a lady passenger keep a watchful eye on Le Manquais as, leaning perilously from his carriage window, he captures ex-LNWR 0–4–2WT No 3249's stately works train progress through Crewe Station with a service wagon and van. One of five such crane-fitted tanks built at Crewe in 1894, the little engine's LNWR number was 853, until March 1895, when it was placed on the Duplicate List as 3249. Still retained by LMSR for Departmental duties at Crewe Works, it kept its duplicate number until it was withdrawn in December 1947.

Well aware of the LNWR/LMSR electric train services which had operated between Euston and Watford since 10 July 1922, Le Manquais later took advantage of a conveniently advertised steam-hauled Saturday afternoon excursion to check on LMSR activities at Richmond, Surrey.

28 August 1937: In the year 1937 Richmond station was an even more exciting place than this juxtaposition of steam and electric trains suggests. The main station, off right, was undergoing vigorous reconstruction in the spirit of Southern Railway electrification. Meanwhile, the long since electrified bays at the north end of the station continued to accommodate LMSR (formerly North London Rly) trains from Broad Street, as they had done from 1 October 1916. The saloon set seen on the left of this photograph is similar to those introduced by the LNWR in 1922 when electric services into Euston commenced. Fitted with Oerlikon electrical equipment, these trains offered comfortable saloon accommodation, though during rush hours, their single end sliding doors were something of a handicap. Nevertheless,

28 August 1937

they soldiered on, until they were replaced by BR standard electric stock in the early 1960s.

The steam locomotive, meanwhile, LMSR 2–6–4T No 2374, having emptied its excursion train, is easing its way out, and will report back later for the return journey to Central London.

Just over a year later Le Manquais, with knowledge aforethought, as one might have guessed, turned up at Bletchley station; and, after photographing several vintage LNWR and L&YR engines which lay outside the adjacent engine shed, took the first cross-country train to Oxford.

17 September 1938: A visit to Oxford station proves well worthwhile. After initial trials between Euston and Tring on 24 March, during which it put up a maximum speed of 85mph, this sleek-looking LMSR hydraulic diesel set, designed by W. A. Stanier, settled down to public service making return trips daily between Oxford and Cambridge. With conventional locomotion requiring three hours, the diesel train ran the 77 miles, with stops at Bletchley, Bedford, and Sandy, in 1¾ hours. The set consisted of three streamlined coaches, numbered 80000–002, with the centre coach 51ft 9in, and the end coaches 63ft 9¾in, long. Each of the latter carried two 125 bhp Leyland diesel engines. Total length of the 73-ton set was 184ft 6in. Each bogie had a 9ft wheelbase, and passenger accommodation was 24 first and 138 third class. Stored at Bedford during the early war years, the set was converted in 1949 into a diesel-powered overhead line maintenance unit for the Manchester, South Junction & Altrincham line. It was last seen in 1969, derelict at Longsight.

17 September 1938

Le Manquais' final LMSR photograph for 1938 recorded yet another facet of surging company pride. This time it involved a visit to Euston Station, where centenary celebrations were being held to commemorate the through opening of the London & Birmingham Railway. Platforms 6 (L&BR's original 'Departure Parade') and 7 were fully occupied by an assembly of locos and rolling stock. *Rocket*, in the shape of a model built by Derby Works, 'Old Coppernob', *Cornwall*, and ex-LNWR 'George V'

19 September 1938

No 5348 *Coronation* featured prominently amongst the historic exhibits. Standing separately, both in steam, *Lion* and *Duchess of Gloucester*, whose namesake opened the Exhibition, offered the ultimate contrast in locomotive development through the ages.

19 September 1938: Built for Liverpool & Manchester Railway, at a cost of £1,100 each, in 1838, 0–4–2s No 57 *Lion* and 58 *Tiger* were the first locomotives to be constructed by Todd, Kitson & Laird of Leeds, later of Kitson & Co fame. Eventually entering LNWR service in 1846, *Lion* was sold for £400 to Mersey Docks & Harbour Board in 1859, and was used for decades as a stationary pumping engine. In 1928 it was rescued from obscurity, and, restored at Crewe Works, it took a very active part in the Liverpool & Manchester Railway centenary celebrations of 1930. *Lion*'s massive companion in this picture, quite recently shopped from Crewe Works, is No 6225 *Duchess of Gloucester*, one of Stanier's celebrated streamlined 'Coronation' Class 'Pacifics'. Only 24 of 38 'Coronation' locomotives built were streamlined, and all lost their distinctive casing in the late 1940s.

To mark the opening of the exhibition, both *Lion* and No 6225 were driven off, midst clouds of vapour, to the station yard. Lord Stamp, Chairman of the LMSR, was at the regulator of the 'Duchess'. *Lion* was handled by the grandson of its builder. We need hardly add that the workaday 2–6–4T seen on the right did *not* form part of the exhibition!

CHAPTER FOUR

LONDON & NORTH EASTERN RAILWAY

My own recollections of the LNER's formation are childish, yet possibly the sharper for that. They centre round my father, an archetypal North British Railway goods guard, whose company pride was eloquently supported by the gold-threaded monogram which graced the lapels of his uniform. He appeared to receive a new uniform annually, and, being both a Scot and careful with his clothes, his habit was to pass discarded railway jackets on to various relatives who laboured, as he once did, on Border country farms. Ergo, the painstaking unpicking of gold thread by my mother, and such other members of the family as could be recruited, was a familiar sight in my childhood days. Then one day, quite suddenly, the comparative flamboyance of the NBR monogram disappeared, and a much more sombre 'LNER' took its place. The letters, in red if I remember rightly, were encircled, totemwise, in a fashion which seemed quite radical at the time.

Even as a boy I was impressed by the ease with which my father slipped into his new role. There were no regrets, no complaints. He still talked proudly of the 'NB', and maintained his long-standing, albeit good-natured, disparagement of all things 'Caledonian'. Our family, too, were still treated to the occasional eulogy on the merits of the NBR 'Superheaters', the Class 'S' 0–6–0s which traditionally ferried him to and fro on his long goods train hauls to Berwick and Carlisle. But times were changing. A year or two later two 'K3' Moguls arrived at Polmont to take over these arduous duties—and within weeks father could be heard to observe, with genuine satisfaction, that 'Gresley seems to build a good engine.'

Conversely, old company rivalries were not forgotten. Opposite us there lived an ex-Caledonian Railway goods guard, John Murray by name. One morning I watched my father stride off to work, in full LNER regalia. He had not proceeded far when, coming *off* duty, who should loom round the corner—but John Murray! He, of course, was dressed as an LMSR goods guard should be. My heart leapt. So, too, did my unbounded curiosity. But I need not have worried. The two men were quite equal to the occasion. John simply crossed to the other side of the street and the two 'friends' passed each other without even a flicker of recognition. At the time I thought it was wonderful. I still do.

Clearly these qualities of loyalty and resilience, particularly when harnessed by undivided management and the benign mechanical leadership of Nigel Gresley, did much to create a 'happy ship' from the moment the LNER set sail on 1 January 1923. Though only second in size in the 'Big Four' hierarchy, its new 'empire' of 6,674 route-miles, 20,156 passenger vehicles, 284,481 freight vehicles, and 15,983 service units posed problems enough, particularly when, of the 7,383 steam locomotives also inherited, nearly one third came from the NER alone. In these circumstances, too, the LNER's appointment of Gresley, a GNR man, as 'Loco Supremo' carried the seeds of potential discord where three major railway works—Doncaster, Stratford, and Darlington—were concerned. It would be idle to pretend that vigorous rivalry did not surface, but, as posterity well knows, it lacked the lethal quality of the Derby-Crewe feud.

Down south, meanwhile, Le Manquais, released from his immediate SR environment by the need to attend daytime studies in Central London, was already discovering that the pulse of LNER affairs in the Metropolis was a degree sharper than a casual visitor might have guessed. Consider the following; a view he snatched during a brief visit to King's Cross in the late winter of 1931.

31 March 1931

31 March 1931: One reason why dense fog used to play such an endemic role in London life. Ex-GNR 'N1' 0–6–2T No 4589 cannot help adding its

quota to the already smokeladen atmosphere around King's Cross as, working flat out, it hoists its South London freight train up and through Hotel
Curve Tunnel. Condensing equipment did so little to alleviate the extreme
discomfort of enginemen on this notorious section of LNER's underground
system that after World War 2 such engine turns were always worked
bunker-first. This at least meant that smoke and steam exhaust fell behind,
rather than in front, and maximum advantage could be taken of the engines'
gravity sanding arrangements. But, even at the best of times, Hotel Curve's
heavily-graded rails could still be as slippery as a basket of eels.

The truth was, of course, that the process of grappling with ever increasing London
suburban traffic had long provided GNR with all the drama it required. Even as a
new century dawned it was plain to see that H. A. Ivatt's gallant little 'Atlantic' tanks
were being overwhelmed and soon their replacement became a matter of urgency. In
the event Ivatt's bold introduction, in 1903, of a giant new 0–8–2T was frustrated by
mandatory weight and size restrictions which governed locomotive operations on
the Metropolitan & City widened lines, and 1907 arrived ere his next suburban design, his Class 'N1' 0–6–2T, finally secured Metropolitan Railway blessing. No less
than 55 more were subsequently turned at Doncaster, and, initially, all but four
worked in the London area.

Ten more years passed, and Ivatt's successor found himself faced with exactly the
same problem—that of providing a fresh solution to the GNR's increasing suburban
workload. The result on this occasion was the emergence, in 1920–21, of Gresley's
ubiquitous 'N2' 0–6–2Ts. Piston-valved, higher boilered, superheated, and significantly more powerful than their Ivatt predecessors, they scored such an immediate
success that they were, in fact, destined to remain in command of King's Cross suburban traffic until the day diesels took over. It follows that 'N2s' formed an integral,
and striking, part of the local scene when Le Manquais paid King's Cross a second
visit in 1933.

5 April 1933: After the briefest of respites 'N2' No 4578 will soon be off
again with another standard load of two quadruple-articulated suburban
sets. The engine was one of fifty supplied by NB Loco Co in 1920–21. The
first ten 'N2s' were built at Doncaster; and once the class was accepted as
standard by the LNER it was augmented by 47 more, from various makers,
between 1925 and 1929.

Twelve of the latter contingent, built by Beyer Peacock, were even de-
spatched to Central Scotland in the spring of 1925. Known to *affecionados*
there as 'Teddy Bears', because of their neat, but powerful, appearance, they
earned a rather less respectful reputation as 'Metropolitans' at the hands of
NBR enginemen, who deemed their footplate amenities 'crude'. Fitters, too,
disliked the engines. Nevertheless, 32 more 'N2s' found their way north by
1929, though 29 made the return trip twelve months later, when Gresley's
much more popular 'V2' 2–6–2Ts arrived on the Scottish scene. Content,
meanwhile, to ignore all this 'N2' activity, No 4758 remained ever faithful
to GN Section, until it was withdrawn as BR No 69537, in April 1959.

5 April 1933 (1)

Another traditional King's Cross feature also occupied Le Manquais' attention. It was the locomotive yard, a shade nearer Gasworks Tunnel, where engines, freshly arrived from King's Cross shed, took up their north-facing stance as they awaited further orders.

5 April 1933 (2)

5 April 1933: Glowing green in late afternoon sunshine, three King's Cross express locomotives are ready for their respective calls. No 4406, one of 94

'C1' 'Atlantics' so proudly introduced by Ivatt thirty years before, will be first to move—and will probably handle a Hitchin, or Cambridge, train. Next in line, 'A1' 'Pacific' No 4471 *Sir Frederick Banbury*, was, of course, one of the famous duo built by the GNR just before Grouping. The engine's rather generous GNR loading gauge proportions were reduced, in common with others, in 1928 to meet LNER requirements.

The square front bufferbeam of the 'Pacific' furthest from the camera not only helps to identify the loco as No 4479 *Robert the Devil*, but recalls an incident on 10 May 1927, when *Victor Wild*, entrusted with a trial run between London and Newcastle, unexpectedly fouled the edge of No 8 Platform at Newcastle Central. Gresley's immediate reaction was to have his 'Pacifics' front footsteps removed, and square front bufferbeams rounded off. A Grantham engine at the time, and one not, therefore, required to work north of York, *Robert the Devil* escaped this treatment for several years, until events overtook it—in late April 1933.

Over on LNER's GC Section, meanwhile, J. G. Robinson had solved *his* company's London suburban problems in 1911 by introducing powerful new 4-6-2Ts in lieu of his earlier 'Atlantic' tanks: 31 were ultimately built at Gorton Works, and, symptomatic of Gresley's generous regard for other men's work, 23 more, now classified 'A5', were added during 1923-26. Despite this, Marylebone station, as Le Manquais discovered during an investigatory visit in 1931, flattered to deceive, with its long periods of inactivity. To obtain a true picture of GCR locomotive activity in Greater London one had to move a little further out—to Neasden. Here, miraculously, only a strip of waste ground separated engine shed and Dog Lane, now part of the North Circular Road.

23 April 1932

23 April 1932: Accessibility apart, another great merit of the former GCR shed at Neasden was that even well into the 1930s its locomotive content remained 100 per cent Great Central. The scene here is typical. Class 'A5' 4-6-2T No 5166 and 'N5' 0-6-2T No 5773 occupy the foreground, while 'B3' 4-6-0 No 6166 *Earl Haig* and an original 'A5', No 5448, complete with GC chimney, bring up the rear. A 'C4' 'Atlantic' can also be seen in the background.

The 'B3' was particularly interesting. Though built at Gorton in 1920, it was the first of its class to be allocated to Neasden—in 1927. Almost immediately it was joined by 6169 *Lord Faringdon*, and the two locomotives maintained their connection with Neasden shed until the end of World War 2. 2. Fitted with Caprotti valve gear at Gresley's instigation in 1929, No 6166 then lost its name in October 1943, when Edward Thompson, bent on furthering the cause of loco standardization, undertook a much more radical rebuild. Unrecognizable thereafter as a former GCR engine, and the only 'B3' to enter BR stock, the one time *Earl Haig* perished quietly, as No 61497, in April 1949.

That visit to Neasden shed was one of few indulgences Le Manquais permitted himself during 1932, for his studies at the Royal College clearly demanded, and were being given, full attention. Still, reward came when success in gaining his BSc provided him with both career and much needed leisure time. Out, then, he went—to Welwyn Garden City. That winter his once familiar Southern Railway ambience soon underwent subtle transformation and by the spring of 1933 he and his camera were ready to focus on LNER main line activity. I warrant one perfect afternoon he spent by the lineside near Potters Bar lingered long, and happily, in his memory.

29 March 1933 (1)

29 March 1933: LNER 'P1' Class 2-8-2 No 2394, one of a pair built in 1925 to meet mineral traffic requirements between Peterborough and Hornsey, looks quite at ease on Potters Bar Up goods line as it passes with its 1,500-ton train. At this juncture the engine was still carrying its Westinghouse pump and undercab booster. The latter, though it raised the tractive effort by 8,500 lb to a total of 47,000 lb, gave much technical trouble, however, not least when attempts to use New England shed's tight turning triangle frequently fractured the steam pipe which passed along the left-hand side of the engine. Eventually, the booster equipment was removed from both 'Mikados' in 1937–38.

Another embarrassment proved to be the very length of the tremendous loads these locomotives were capable of hauling. This sorely harassed the Operating Department, and long delays were often experienced, particularly with Up coal trains. Frequent restarts consequently increased coal consumption, and, all in all, the withdrawal of both 'P1s' in July 1945 came as no great surprise.

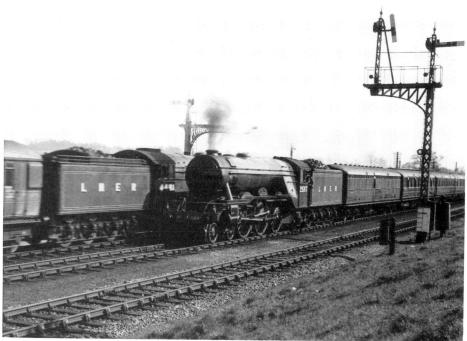

29 March 1933 (2)

29 March 1933: In this opportunist meeting of Gresley 'Pacifics' near Potters Bar No 2597 *Gainsborough* is heading a Down express bound for Newcastle, while No 4481 *St Simon*, almost seven years its senior, hurries south towards King's Cross. *Gainsborough* is carrying a New Type non-corridor tender, and the older engine still retains its original GNR type with coal rails. 4481 did, in fact, receive a streamlined non-corridor tender in May 1937, but eleven months later was obliged to revert to the old type. No 2597 stayed with the tender originally allocated to it.

29 March 1933: 'K3' 2-6-0 No 170 makes an impressive sight as it heads through Potters Bar with its Down express goods. After Grouping Gresley

29 March 1933 (3)

adopted this well-proven GNR class for further development, and No 170, Darlington-built in March 1925, was one of 183 built between 1924 and 1927 to LNER Composite Loading Gauge. Hardworking engines, they were popular in every LNER Region. Practically all saw 1960 in, and No 170, by then BR No 61851, was withdrawn in November 1961. Her elegant appearance is well matched in the above scene by classic GNR somersault signals.

A year or two later, still vigilant by the lineside, Le Manquais captured another intriguing LNER type.

22 August 1936

22 August 1936: Around the mid-1920s ex-GER 'Clauds', running *via* Hitchin, established a useful reputation for themselves on King's Cross-Cambridge duties, and when, in May 1932, the LNER decided to experiment boldly by initiating five new express trains each weekday between Cambridge and King's Cross, 'Clauds' again found favour in working these comparatively light trains. Carrying buffet cars, and popularly known as 'Beer Trains', one such is seen in our picture, with No 8899 striding out for London.

The 'Claud Hamiltons', a class of 111 extremely elegant 4–4–0s built at Stratford Works in 1900–11, with ten more added in 1923, had already been the subject of development by GER; and the principle was taken up wholeheartedly by Gresley after Grouping. Consequently, three initial LNER classifications, 'D14', 'D15', and 'D16', soon acquired sub-categories. No 8899, for instance, originally a saturated 'D15', graduated as a 'D15/2' by 1925, and went on to acquire a GNR chimney eleven years later. Most 'Clauds' worked on into the 1950s, as did 8899, which was withdrawn, bearing No 62510, in October 1957.

Once he settled in at Welwyn, weekend leisure soon allowed Le Manquais to take an interest in LNER's GE Section. In the autumn of 1934, for instance, Whitemoor Yard and locomotive shed drew him to March, whence he returned home *via* Peterborough.

23 September 1934: Full of nostalgia, this panoramic railway view was taken from the west end of March station. The line to Peterborough forks off left,

23 September 1934

while metals bending right offer a route to trains bound for Spalding or King's Lynn. Today, March station remains remarkably true to its original appearance, but the complex of metals at its west end has, inevitably, been grossly simplified.

A year later he seized a rare opportunity to travel over former Colne Valley & Halstead Railway metals, when the LNER advertised a Sunday excursion from Marks Tey to Haverhill (South) and back. Nine coaches were required, and the train was hauled by ex-GER 'J15' 0–6–0 No 7523. In the absence of photo-stops *en route*, Le Manquais, true to his craft, shrewdly positioned himself in the last carriage, a conveniently rear-windowed saloon. Thus, once the excursion entered CV&HR territory at Chappel & Wakes Colne, views of White Colne, Halstead, and Yeldham stations fell happily to his camera.

Incorporated in 1856, CV&HR opened its first six miles of single line to Halstead four years later. Significantly, three more years elapsed before it reached its goal at Haverhill. During the company's 67 years of independent existence never a passenger fatality occurred, but neither, alas, was there a dividend paid on ordinary shares. Thus, wearied additionally by fierce bus competition after World War 1, the CV&HR was not sorry to be absorbed as an LNER subsidiary company on 1 January 1923. Only two of its four tank engines lived to carry LNER numbers.

3 November 1935 (1)

3 November 1935: Once the scene of bustling activity, now an empty shell, CV&HR's workshops (left) at Halstead became the 'nerve centre' in 1908, when the Locomotive & Engineering Department was transferred from Haverhill. As can be seen, Colne Valley's Halstead establishment allowed itself plenty of elbow room. The yard was spacious, and supplies of (rather hard) water were drawn from a deep well in front of the stationmaster's office.

Reaction was swift, however, once LNER took over in 1923. Passenger rolling stock was withdrawn, the workshops at Halstead were first denuded of machinery, then demolished, and the process of conversion from flat-bottomed to bull-headed rail, already begun by CV&HR, was completed. Even so, the existence of weak bridges along the line restricted LNER choice of motive power to ex-GER 'J15' 0–6–0s, with their modest axle loading—until Ivatt 2–6–0s arrived in 1951.

3 November 1935 (2)

3 November 1935: Having worked its heavy excursion train all the way from Marks Tey, 'J15' No 7523 rests quietly in CV&HR's old engine shed at Haverhill. Haverhill South station (behind the loco shed) was closed to passenger traffic on 24 July 1924, and branch trains, thereafter employing a link which was established between CV&HR and GER in 1865, ran through to Haverhill North. The goods depot at Haverhill South was, however, retained by the LNER—witness the goods shed and wagons seen right—and, indeed, during World War 2 White Colne and Earls Colne stations, because of their proximity to US Army airfields, handled a heavy flow of ammunition traffic. In post-war years road transport won the inevitable battle, and the old CV&HR line was closed down completely on 1 January 1962.

Another branch line which aroused Le Manquais' interest was obliged to close ten years earlier, in September 1952. Once again, bus competition delivered the death blow, and soon the last remnants of the one time Elsenham & Thaxted Light Railway vanished from sight. In 1936, however, the 5½-mile GER branch was still running, under LNER auspices. As always, its light construction, steep gradients, and numerous curves combined to impose a 14-ton maximum axle loading. As a consequence both LNER and BR followed GER example by employing 'Buckjumpers', the ex-GER 0–6–0 suburban tanks of immortal fame.

15 August 1936

15 August 1936: Ex-GER 'J69/1' 0–6–0T No 7193 brings its Thaxted branch train into Henham Halt, and the guard hovers politely as a group of villagers see a friend off to the main line at Elsenham, 1½ miles distant. Note the steps which were fitted for passenger use at the low-platformed halts. Even the carriage wheels on Thaxted branch stock were reduced to 2ft 9in diameter from 3ft 6½in. The coach nearest the camera, brake third No 62913, and passenger third No 60866 were two of five six-wheeled vehicles specially converted at Stratford Works for the opening of the branch on 1 April 1913. The pair served faithfully right up to 21 June 1947. They even lived on another seventeen years as service units before meeting their doom in 1964.

In the year 1936 three oil lamps, a garden seat, an old coach acting as waiting room, and a fire bucket offered such sophistication as Henham Halt could summon. Yet there is a timeless charm about this country station scene. Only too typical of modern times, it vanished when BR closed the 'Gin & Toffee' line on 15 September 1952.

We move now, further north, to NER territory. How right David Joy was when he recorded in his (September 1889) diary—'That lovely York station, which always gives me the idea of being pleasure bent!' I loved York station. Like Carlisle, it had all the mystique of inter-company rivalry and still-throbbing memories of the 'Race to the North'. Patently, Le Manquais, too, was impressed as can be judged by the photographs he took one Saturday afternoon, when he lingered there before pressing on overnight for Edinburgh.

6 June 1936 (1)

6 June 1936: Beautifully liveried in LNER green, ex-GCR B4 4-6-0 No 6101 backs proudly on to its Scarborough train at the north end of York Station. Ten of these handsome engines were built by Beyer Peacock & Co in 1906, and the third-built, named *Immingham*, was the first GCR 4-6-0 to be so honoured. Originally designed to handle express goods and fish traffic on the GCR system, these Robinson locomotives were displaced latterly on main line service by newer types, and after Grouping they wandered widely on both GE and GN Sections. No 6101 was one of five 'B4s' allocated to Copley Hill shed during the mid-1930s, and it was still in the West Riding area, at Ardsley, when it was withdrawn, as LNER No 1486, in October 1947. The last of the class followed suit three years later.

6 June 1936: Dramatically framed by the forest of signals which hallmarked the southern approach to York Station, ex-NER 'B16' 4-6-0 No 2380 arrives with a very mixed ten-coach 'special' for Scarborough. At Grouping NER handed over 38 of these trim-looking Raven locos, and 32 more, again built at Darlington, were added by LNER in 1923–24. Popular, hard-working engines, only their mixed traffic designation denied them the privilege of green livery.

6 June 1936 (2)

Soon after one 'B16' was destroyed during an air raid on York in April
1942, NE Area took the extraordinary step of concentrating the remaining
69, including seven which had been rebuilt with Walschaerts valve gear by
Gresley, at York. This wartime measure, aimed at easing maintenance and
facilitating supply of spare parts, lasted until 1949, when many 'B16s' were
again released to handle their customary spectrum of duties elsewhere on
ex-NER territory. Withdrawals commenced in 1958, and No 2380,
unrebuilt to the end, perished, as BR No 61451, in September 1961.

With his sharp eye for 'events', Le Manquais attended an even more nostalgic exhibition one year later.

6 June 1937

6 June 1937: A perennial favourite at LNER Exhibitions all through the 1930s, ex-GER 'Y5' 0–4–0ST No 7230, is seen here at Stratford Works, together with a beautifully restored Eastern Counties Railway saloon. Known to all and sundry as the 'Coffee Pot', the little saddletank was one of a final pair built at Stratford in 1903 as a modification of earlier Neilson & Co locos. The only survivor of eight by 1931, No 7230 carried on as Stratford Carriage Works shunter, until it was withdrawn in April 1948. The Westinghouse pump and cylindrical air reservoir, fitted in 1916, were relics of carriage testing days; and the unusual pipe leading from the right-hand side of the chimney drew off exhaust from the loco's vacuum ejector. The immaculate condition of both engine and carriage, meanwhile, speaks volumes for LNER pride.

So, too, did three more locos which were photographed over the next fifteen months.

17 September 1937

17 September 1937: Fully liveried in standard LNER green, York engine 'V2' No 4773 looks incorrigibly handsome as it awaits further instructions at Doncaster station. The engine was, in fact, less than a year old, for it emerged from Doncaster Works (Works No 1843) as one of five prototype engines in October 1936. The continuing success of Gresley's new mixed traffic design never faltered; and every main line shed, from Aberdeen to King's Cross, welcomed its quota from the 184 ultimately built. Class performance was masterly on every type of work during World War 2 despite deplorable maintenance conditions.

In 1953, when all thirty Merchant Navy 'Pacifics' had to be withdrawn for axle examination, and other regions had to assist, BR's Eastern Region intriguingly lent six 'V2s'! Despite being unfamiliar to Southern Region men who handled them, they acquitted themselves well, before returning to normal pastures a month or two later. Ten years later, when insufficient diesel locos were available to man GN section main line duties, 'V2s' again made a name for themselves. No 4773 was withdrawn as BR No 60802 in March 1964, but, fittingly, No 4771 *Green Arrow*, the class prototype, survived to earn inclusion in the National Railway Museum collection.

19 June 1938

19 June 1938: Had it not been a Sunday morning, 'A4' No 2510 *Quicksilver* would have attracted much more attention as it strolled into Welwyn Garden City station on a Down local. Second of four streamlined 'Pacifics' built at Doncaster in 1935 specifically to handle LNER's new 'Silver Jubilee' service, and still strikingly liveried in grey, *Quicksilver* also stood in as required when the even tougher 'Coronation' high-speed service evolved in 1937. Possibly its appearance at Welwyn on humbler duties meant the loco was being 'run in' after mechanical attention at Doncaster. No one could have guessed that sister engine *Mallard* would log a new world steam speed record of 126 mph exactly a fortnight later! Renumbered 60015 by BR, *Quicksilver* was cut up at Doncaster in 1963. Apart from a very brief flirtation with Gateshead shed in December 1936, it remained a Southern Section engine for the whole of its working life.

17 September 1938: Construction in 1936–37 of 25 more LNER 'B17' 4–6–0s, with larger 4,200-gallon flat-sided tenders, brought many more of these handsome engines into former GCR areas: hence this study of No

17 September 1938

2850 *Grimsby Town*, by now a Woodford loco, on express passenger duty at Banbury. The curved nameplate, with its 8½in gilded football replica and black and white enamelled splasher, must have raised many a GWR eyebrow! Popular, but rough runners, the 'B17s' were only too soon supplanted by 'Pacifics' and 'V2s'; and eventually *Grimsby Town*, with many others, found its way back to the GE Section, original haunt of the class in 1928. Renumbered 61650 by BR, the engine was withdrawn from Stratford shed in September 1958. That same year a completely rebuilt Banbury Station resumed operations with four through lines.

A rather different selection of locomotives came the LNER's way on 1 October 1936, when the major company acquired control of the Midland & Great Northern Joint Railway. Like GNSR in the north of Scotland, M&GNJR had long pinned its passenger traffic faith in the use of 4–4–0s; thus, it came as no surprise that sixty locos of that type were present amongst the 85 engines initially proffered to the LNER. After selective withdrawal of twenty vintage 4–4–0s and five 0–6–0s, the LNER, in 1937, finally accepted sixty M&GN locomotives.

Traditionally, M&GN engines which worked around Peterborough had always found a haven in the Midland Railway's old shed at Spital Bridge. Now, under LNER auspices, such engines were transferred to Peterborough East. But New England shed also harboured a quota; as Le Manquais found when his southbound train paused one day opposite that august institution.

17 October 1937: The close proximity of two GER 'J15s' serves to emphasize the classic MR lines of 4–4–0 No 043. Designed at Derby by S. W.

17 October 1937

Johnson, it was one of 26 class 'C' engines delivered by Sharp Stewart to M&GNR in 1894. Seven more followed in 1896, and Beyer Peacock brought the class total to forty three years later. Some acquired larger boilers, and others Belpaire fireboxes, during the early 1900s. Certainly all worked hard for the next forty years as they carried the brunt of M&GN passenger traffic: so much so, that seventeen class 'Cs' were part of the twenty aging 4–4–0s rejected by LNER in 1937. Those taken into stock were classified as 'D52', '53', or '54', according to their stage of development. No 043, one of few 'D52s' left after November 1937, contrived to retain its small Johnson boiler until the day it was withdrawn in June 1943.

Speaking of locomotive development, once 2–4–2Ts in their final form with radial axle boxes began to emerge from Crewe, T. W. Worsdell, a past pupil of Webb's, decided in 1884 to build the type for GER. Improvements were gradually incorporated, and, so useful did the tanks prove on suburban and branch work, that no fewer than 242 were built at Stratford over the years to 1912. There were five classes in all, and 232 of these versatile locos, handed over at Grouping, constituted two-thirds of LNER's total intake of 2–4–2Ts in 1923. Scrapping proceeded fairly steadily over the next fifteen years, but many were still about when Le Manquais began to take an interest in former GER branches. One, the Buntingford branch, even offered the interested observer a choice of three ex-GER 2–4–2T types, now LNER classes 'F4', 'F5', and 'F6'.

28 June 1938: Despite vigorous opposition from sundry vested interests, including Eastern Counties Railway, a Bill founding the Ware, Hadham & Buntingford railway received Royal Assent on 12 July 1858. Predictably, five

28 June 1938

years of weary negotiation followed, and when, on 10 February 1863, an inaugural train of shareholders left Bishopsgate station, headed by ECR 2–4–0 No 182, those aboard who were not *au fait* with current developments discovered one hour later that the proposed 'branch from Ware' actually bypassed that town, by hiving off from the main line at St Margarets, which station served the smaller community of Stanstead Abbots. Still, on they went, now observing a branch restriction speed of 20 mph, and, another 45 minutes and 13½ miles later, Buntingford residents, assembled at a flag-bedecked station, afforded them a right royal welcome. Over-optimism, meanwhile, had led to near-bankruptcy on the original sponsors' part, and before public services commenced on 3 July 1863 prudent arrangements had to be made for the newly-formed Great Eastern Railway to work the branch.

So lightly was the branch constructed, GER employed a variety of small tank engines over the years. Early in the new century 2–4–2Ts, known initially as 'Gobblers' (though subsequent reconstruction removed their defect, if not their nickname) began to monopolize Buntingford branch services. Then, around 1932, three LNER class 'F6' 2–4–2Ts arrived on the local scene. Windows in their cab side-sheets readily distinguished them from their predecessors. They functioned comfortably enough until class 'N7' 0–6–2Ts took over in 1949. 'F6' No 7002, pictured here at Buntingford station, later became BR No 67231. Stratford-built in 1911, it was finally withdrawn by BR in March 1958. Buntingford branch, with its six intermediate stations, fared little better: long subjected to bus competition, passenger services thereon terminated on 14 November 1964, and a last freight train ran ten months later. Station buildings were soon reduced to heaps of rubble, and the once proud site of Buntingford station is now a housing estate. Rather wanly, chained Bibles which were provided, in accordance with GER tradition, at every signal box on the branch, lingered through the years, until 1960, when the last was removed.

Fortunately, Le Manquais' avid awareness of LNER matters enables us to close both 1938 and this chapter on a much more cheerful note. It centres round a very special visit he paid to King's Cross one Sunday morning later that year.

11 September 1938

11 September 1938: Built in 1870, and destined to handle many an East Coast express in her day, GNR single-wheeler No 1 was a supreme example of Patrick Stirling's craft. The engine was withdrawn in 1907, but, thanks in the main to Nigel Gresley's refusal to see her scrapped, found a secure niche twenty years later in LNER's Railway Museum at York. On the introduction of a new 'Flying Scotsman' train in June 1928, LNER management had a stroke of inspiration—and out came the old lady, to make several excursions heading a rake of vintage Great Northern Railway stock. Equally inspired, the Railway Correspondence & Travel Society promptly commissioned the loco for Britain's very first enthusiasts' rail tour. Thus, three months later, No 1 again ferried her vintage stock, and 170 enthusiasts, from King's Cross to Peterborough and back. As can be seen from this King's Cross photograph the event sparked off considerable public interest. Note, too, the comparative absence of cameras that innocent year. Meanwhile, quietly ignored for once, Gresley's masterpiece of 1935, No 2509 *Silver Link*, simmered away gracefully, on an adjacent platform (off left), at the head of a modern LNER northbound express!

CHAPTER FIVE

GREAT WESTERN RAILWAY

The Great Western always was a rather patrician concern. All through its history it had quietly absorbed smaller companies as it steadily forged a near-monopoly of metals throughout the West of England; and it came as no surprise that, when the time came, it faced Grouping with an equanimity others of the 'Big Four' did not, or could not, share. The main reason, of course, was that GWR was not called upon to sacrifice either identity, independence, or individuality. Life at Swindon would go on much as before—except that the family was now a little larger.

Seen now in retrospect, quite a few aspects of GWR's good fortune offer illuminating comparison with events 'elsewhere'. To begin with, the six major Welsh railways who allied themselves with the old GWR contributed such a minor proportion of assets and revenue to the common weal that GWR management was left not only free, but totally justified, in retaining command; a vastly different circumstance from the Derby/Crewe situation. Again, Swindon, with its long and distinguished record of locomotive development, did not require the advent of a Nigel Gresley, or a W. A. Stanier, to thrash out new policies of locomotive standardization. C. B. Collett, a disciple of, and worthy successor to, the great G. J. Churchward, had already slipped quietly into office. Thirdly, GWR faced none of the suburban electrification problems which so preoccupied the newly-formed Southern Railway.

Another helpful factor in minimizing trauma was that the provisions of the 1921 Railway Act were taken up more swiftly in the West. Thus, twelve months before the official date of Amalgamation dawned on 1 January 1923, the new GWR had already licked itself into shape; and was able to present a *fait accompli* of seven constituent companies ie, those entitled to nominate directors to the new Board, and thirteen subsidiary companies. The latter complement even managed to double itself by 1 July 1923. But, as can be seen from the Table which follows, Paddington still held the reins.

GREAT WESTERN RAILWAY – 1923

	GWR – Main Constituent Company	Six (Welsh) constituent companies added on 1st Jan 1922	26 Subsidiary companies added 1922–23
Issued Capital	£101 million	£29.23 million	£15.39 million
Net Income for 1921	£6,188,433	£1,491,649	£497,664
Total Route Miles	2,784	473	460
Locomotives	3,148	713	184
Passenger Carriages	5,581	831	252
Freight Wagons	88,755	9,081	1,270

Subsequent events on the GWR have been well chronicled. Suffice it to say that the more elderly locomotives bequeathed by the minor Companies were either scrapped or placed on the sales list by the end of 1926. The bulk of the remainder, some 700 engines, were painstakingly overhauled at Swindon over the same four-year period; and re-emerged, reboilered as likely as not, to enter a new phase of working life. Full marks to Swindon, it would appear.

Yet, it was precisely this relentless process of standardization which provoked a curious ambivalence in the heart of many a provincial observer. Speaking personally, I found Paddington Station in the year 1934 a rather less exciting place than I had anticipated. Indeed, the first GWR engine I ever set eyes on—a 'Castle' freshly arrived from Bristol—gave me quite a shock, particularly as I had also seen my first 'Lord Nelson' at Waterloo the day before. Somehow I expected something much more massive than this beautifully-proportioned creature! The dark Brunswick of her green livery too, seemed unnecessarily sombre to me. Then the same locomotive backed out—and reproached me, as her chimney, dome and splashers gloried in the morning sun . . .

I was to learn, of course, as the day went on that gentle lines belied great power as far as GWR express locos were concerned. They had, too, a crispness of exhaust which was quite new to my Scottish ears. 'Castles' and 'Stars' barked their way out of

Paddington, handling heavy loads quite effortlessly. I closed my eyes, and the sound was that of wood being chopped. But one thing is certain; the way in which GWR serviced the whole West of England from this one comparatively modest station quite staggered me. Train after train rolled in; and within minutes pannier tanks buffered up, empty coaches were whipped out, and new trains took their place.

Strictly speaking, Le Manquais was no 'provincial'. Yet, patently, the formative years he spent south of the Thames insulated him fairly effectively from GWR activities. Early photographs suggest that only an occasional Dean 0–6–0 or 0–4–2T ever frequented his favourite boyhood vantage point at Clapham Junction. Even as late as 1934 journeys over GWR metals to and from Fishguard in pursuit of an Irish holiday were undertaken in the evening: hence his camera remained in its case. Later that year, however, came clear evidence that he had kept himself well abreast of current GWR developments, for, after a long apprenticeship with steam rail motors and auto-train working, the GWR finally embraced diesel-engined propulsion. Le Manquais, curious to witness this new phenomenon, hastened out to Reading.

6 October 1934

6 October 1934: GWR's prototype diesel railcar is seen here entering Reading station from Slough. The first of 38 such cars eventually acquired, No 1, built by AEC Ltd of Southall, with bodywork by Park Royal Coachworks Ltd, was tested initially on local duties around Reading from 4 December 1933. Taken out of service for modification, it then returned to the locality on 5 February 1934. The 63½ft long car could be driven from either end, power came from a single 121 bhp diesel engine and electric light was provided throughout. Inside, two passenger compartments seated 69 people, back to back in bus fashion, and, as can be seen, GWR's famous crest occupied a prominent position on the car's beautifully streamlined body. Curiously, although empty weight at 24 tons was considerably less than that of a final batch of eighteen cars taken into GWR stock in 1940–41, the latter, weighing 35 tons and upward, only exceeded No 1's overall length by just over 2ft.

Next camera contact with GWR came seven months later, when what appears to have been a quick weekend trip to the north-west deposited Le Manquais on Shrewsbury Station platforms one Sunday morning.

26 May 1935

26 May 1935: All metals seen in this view of Shrewsbury General Station's south end junction were operated jointly by the LMSR and GWR. The lines inclining left of the signal box ran to Wellington, 10½ miles away. Part of a through route to Stafford and Birmingham, they were opened as far back as 1849. Those going off right got as far as Ludlow in 1852, and were extended to Hereford (56 miles) one year later. It is a sad reflection on modern railway times that, where twenty intermediate stations still existed on these two routes at Grouping, only four remain open today.

Shrewsbury Abbey, gazing benignly on in the background to the right of the box, knew all about the vagaries of railway existence; for, immediately behind it, Shropshire & Montgomeryshire Light Railway's Abbey Station was also fighting a desperate battle for survival.

Back in the metropolis, meanwhile, one of the more beguiling features of north-west London life at that time was the comparative proximity of four major locomotive sheds. We shall never know how many railway enthusiasts, including myself, cheerfully found their way round that parabola, now part of the North Circular Road, which encompassed them in the 1930s. Conversely, there is no indication that Le Manquais ever undertook the 'Grand Tour', but clearly a visit he made to the Old Oak Common vicinity one Saturday in 1935 made a deep impression. After photographing a passing train or two he seems, somehow, to have nudged himself nearer the real centre of operations.

10 August 1935 (1)

10 August 1935: Notwithstanding ample evidence of GWR fittings, No 3028's alien pedigree cannot be concealed. The loco was, in fact, one of 521 GCR-type 2–8–0s which were built by a number of makers during the later stages of World War 1, for use by the Railway Operating Division of the Royal Engineers. Many served in France, others remained in the UK, but all were familiarly known as 'RODs'. Once hostilities ceased, the government undertook the long term task of disposing of these engines. Some were sold abroad, 273 went to the LNER, 75 to the LMSR; and the GWR, having already purchased twenty in 1919, at £10,000 apiece new, and hired 84 more over the next three years, bought a final batch of eighty, at £1,500 each secondhand, in 1925.

As the class was only fitted with steam brake, it is highly probable that No 3028 had reported back to Old Oak Common shed after bringing in an unfitted freight train from Bristol or Reading. This engine was one of 45 'RODs' which lasted until BR days.

10 August 1935: The noble proportions of No 6009 *King Charles II* deserve more than the admiration of a few locomen as the engine poses proudly at Old Oak Common. Introduced at a time when each member of the 'Big Four' was striving for the Blue Riband, as it were, the 'Kings' thrust before the railway world in 1927 a fascinating new blend of Churchward tradition

10 August 1935 (2)

and modern non-standard design. Devotees of Gresley 'Pacifics', 'Royal Scots', and 'Lord Nelsons' found it very hard to accept that a 'King', with its apparently more modest boiler and generously proportioned chimney, could generate a nominal tractive effort of 40,300 lb—and was, theoretically at least, 'the most powerful passenger engine in Britain'!

North Americans were similarly nonplussed when *King George V*, the class prototype, was sent to USA in the latter half of 1927 as Britain's contribution to the Baltimore & Ohio Railroad's centenary celebrations. Trophies in the form of commemorative medals and a B&O locomotive bell are still carried proudly by No 6000 to this day. *King Charles II*, not quite so fortunate, was withdrawn by BR in May 1956.

10 August 1935: Coal in, ash out! No 8390, seen here participating in the daily routine at Old Oak Common, represented an interesting latter-day variation of the '43XX' Class 2–6–0s originally introduced by Churchward in 1911. So successful was this tender version of his '3150' Class 2–6–2T, no fewer than 384 were ultimately built. The uniform design of these highly versatile engines, however, called for modification in the mid-1920s, when it was found that those working in severely curved areas suffered considerably from flange wear on the leading coupled wheels. Swindon's remedy was to lengthen the front buffer beam by one foot (as seen below), and instal a two-ton casting behind it. This had the desired effect of reducing wear; though the increased weight of the 65 locos modified thus, now renumbered '83XX', confined them to work on 'Red' routes. A subsequent shortage of suitable light locomotives for 'Blue' routes obliged a reversal of policy in the 1940s, when 53 surviving '83XXs' were restored to their former condition. The engine in our picture duly ranged the gamut. Built as

10 August 1935 (3)

No 5390 in October 1920, it was renumbered 8390 in March 1928, acquired outside steam pipes in August 1941, reverted to No 5390 in September 1944, and was finally withdrawn by BR in August 1958.

There is something about these Old Oak Common photographs which persuades me that, in keeping with my own experience, Le Manquais' attitude to things Great Western underwent respectful conversion that afternoon. I wonder, though, how he reacted when a rather more exuberant example of GWR enterprise crossed his bows at Paddington exactly one week later!

17 August 1935

17 August 1935: No 5005 *Manorbier Castle* enlivens spectators and dull weather alike as she leaves Paddington for Bristol. Certainly this 'Castle' reshaped by Swindon was an odd sight. A bullet-shaped nose had been super-imposed on her normally conventional smokebox, and, below that, steam chest, cylinder casings, and steampipe had been fused into one air-smoothed mass. At higher level, cowlings fitted behind both chimney and safety valve continued the rather absurd process, and the broad shoulders of the engine's Belpaire firebox were now concealed. Even the front of 5005's cab was wedge-shaped, *coup-de-vent* fashion, and broad metal sheeting over the tender purported to complete the streamlined effect. Lastly, and a surprising touch, a straight nameplate now took precedence over the high curve so beloved by Swindon.

Was it all, one wonders, a half-hearted attempt on the GWR's part to pre-empt the impact of the streamlined 'Pacifics' Gresley was about to release on a fascinated public; or did Swindon already know the truth—that streamlining mattered little, except at very high speeds?

No doubt *Manorbier Castle* functioned as admirably as ever in her new form; but by November that year Swindon grew tired of the experiment. 5005 and *King Henry VII*, another engine similarly maltreated, were pulled in, and all casing round the cylinders and motion was removed. Air smoothing, it appeared, far from assisting, tended to cause the motion to overheat, for at speed the normal flow of cold air was impeded. Gradually, over a period of years other 'extras' were eliminated, and by 1949 all but a faint trace of this rather bizarre Swindon experiment vanished from human ken. *Manorbier Castle*, restored to normal, carried on to serve BR until February 1950.

However he was affected by what he had seen, Le Manquais still made sure that Great Western venues featured quite prominently in his subsequent wanderings. That same day, in fact, he, too, moved on towards Bristol and points west.

18 August 1935

18 August 1935: Far beneath Clifton Suspension Bridge, a GWR train can be seen wending its way towards Portishead. Originally broad-gauge, this single line opened between Bristol, Bedminster, and Portishead on 30 April 1879, and was worked by Bristol & Exeter Railway until that company was vested in GWR five years later. Work on the suspension bridge itself commenced in 1836, but came to a premature halt two years later; much to the disappointment of its designer, Isambard Kingdom Brunel. Brunel died in 1859, and the Institute of Civil Engineers, considering a suitable memorial, colluded with two eminent Members, W. H. Barlow and John Hawkshaw, in arranging purchase of chains and working parts from another Brunel bridge, at Hungerford, London, which was about to be converted into a railway bridge. These components, costing £5,000, were used to complete Clifton Suspension Bridge, which finally opened on 8 December 1864.

Subsequent incursion in Monmouthshire was interesting; for instead of plunging on into South Wales, with its tempting railway ramifications, Le Manquais elected to turn east at Severn Tunnel Junction, and head for Chepstow. There, once more, his patent regard for Brunel and his works found expression, as he made his way to the platform end and trained his camera on the tubular girder bridge built by that remarkable man across the River Wye. Completed in 1852, and since, of course, rebuilt, it served as a prototype for Brunel's even more famous Albert Bridge at Saltash. Thence, striking north, our traveller aimed for Monmouth.

19 August 1935

19 August 1935: Having crossed the viaduct over the River Wye, a GWR auto-train, propelled, almost inevitably, by a standard 0–4–2T, enters Monmoth (Troy) Station from Chepstow. The driver can just be seen in the control cabin. Note, too, the large warning gong above the windscreen, operated by foot pedal and considered necessary despite the fact that the locomotive whistle could be manipulated remotely by overhead wire. A second auto-train can be seen in the left background, alongside the single line which led to Ross-on-Wye. Yet, despite this apparent activity, the whole Wye Valley Junction branch, from Chepstow to Monmouth, was later closed to traffic, from 5 January 1959. Metals behind the camera, leading to Pontypool Road, were closed even earlier to passenger traffic, in May 1955, though a workmen's service to Glascoed ROF lingered on until 24 April 1961.

Having reached the fringe of Severn & Wye territory, and found it to his liking, Le Manquais next turned south for Lydney, the one-time heartland of the Severn & Wye Railway & Canal Company. Here was Great Western history, if you like; for, as long ago as 1813, horses drawing crude 3ft 6in gauge tramroad wagons filled with Forest of Dean coal had trodden the same path. Gradually, over the years the thirty miles of primitive track widened to 3ft 8in. Then, in 1853, Severn & Wye shareholders opted for steam locomotion. Under pressure from the GWR, broad-gauge track was introduced in 1868, but within five years standard-gauge became the order of the day. Then, when the Severn Bridge Railway Company opened its famous bridge in 1879, the two companies merged to form the Severn & Wye and Severn Bridge Railway Company. Four years later a receiver was appointed, and the undertaking was purchased jointly by the Midland and the GWR.

How he travelled, I know not; but Le Manquais arrived at the GWR's Lydney Junction Station that afternoon. There the adjacent level crossing of ex-Severn & Wye freight metals to Lydney Docks and GWR's main line to Cardiff so intrigued him that, after photographing the station, he wandered on towards 'Dockland'.

13 August 1936

13 August 1936: Lydney Harbour was but a poor shadow of its former self when this photograph was taken. The building to the right of the crane, behind the empty GWR wagon, dated from 1813, when a canal was built between Lydney and the River Severn. The South Wales Railway ventured as far as Lydney level crossing in 1853, lines to the Upper Basin of the Canal following in 1872, and by 1897 Lydney Harbour was handling 265,000 tons of coal per annum. Nine coal tips and three cranes were kept busy. In 1927 two tips for small vessels at the top of the canal were dismantled. The process continued over the next decade, and in our photograph two of the few remaining out-harbour tips can be seen. The coal wagons on the left, waiting to be unloaded, will be dealt with the hard way! As their private title indicates, they have come from Norchard, a large colliery a mile or two inland. Owned by Park Colliery Co Ltd, it was the only Forest of Dean pit which did not lie under Crown land.

In the event, an accident to the Severn Bridge on the night of 25 October 1960 brought an end to Lydney Harbour workings, and the British Transport Commission closed down the whole installation one month later.

Holidays in Holland and Scotland kept Le Manquais and his camera busy enough during the first half of 1936. Then, suddenly, with never a hint in his notebook as to how he got there, we find him in Cornwall! He took surprisingly few photographs on what must have been a very quick trip. But he had clearly briefed himself on local railway history, for the Redruth area drew him immediately.

Despite the dreadful state of public roads at the turn of the 18th century, the sheltered port of Hayle, on Cornwall's northern coast, had long known the benefit of horse-drawn import/export trade. The unqualified success of the Redruth & Chasewater Railway, also horse-drawn, convinced other mine owners in the locality in 1826 that they should act similarly—only, this time with steam locomotion. Accordingly, Royal Assent to a proposed Hayle Railway Company Bill was granted on 27 June 1834, and on 11 June 1838 a 9½-mile standard gauge main line between Hayle and Redruth opened to mineral traffic only. Several additional steep inclines, to mines at Roskear, North Crofty, and Tresavean, and to the port of Portreath, brought the Railway's total length to seventeen miles.

Five years later, Hayle Railway directors, fired by GWR's success in inaugurating a passenger service between Paddington and Bristol, resolved they would do their bit for Cornwall. Thus, it was announced that the company's first exclusively *passenger* train would leave Redruth station for Hayle at 9.00 am on the morning of 22 May 1843. To celebrate the occasion, the public were offered free travel—and, such was the response, that three open wagons, packed with excited humanity, had to be added to the two modest carriages initially provided! Even then, only the late arrival of the horsedrawn 'omnibus' from Truro prevented a greater clamour for accommodation. 1¼ hours later, after what were described at the time as 'frightful descents of steep inclines at Penponds and Angarrack', the train arrived at Copperhouse. There the engine was uncoupled, and horses hauled the train over the drawbridge to Hayle Foundry. Three round trips were made that day, and it was anticipated that 45 minutes could safely be allowed for normal service trains.

28 August 1936 (1)

28 August 1936: Now only a coal yard, Hayle Railway's original station at Redruth lay just outside the town when it was built. It takes an effort of imagination to appreciate that, nearly a hundred years before this photograph was taken, trains for Hayle left here daily at 9.00 am, 12 noon, and 5.00 pm; and the last train of the day reported back from Hayle at 6.45 pm. Hayle Railway directors were, in fact, so encouraged by initial success that they proceeded to develop a brisk trade in excursion traffic. Sunday School outings were particularly popular. Fortunately, despite the hazardous inclines which had to be surmounted, the safety record was good.

28 August 1936 (2)

28 August 1936: Tresavean Incline, another relic of Hayle Railway days, was opened, purely for mineral traffic, on 23 June 1838. Half a mile long at 1 in 15, and double-tracked, it lay on a 2½-mile branch off Redruth Junction, and was worked by continuous wire rope which ran over wheels set 7 or 8 yards apart in the middle of each track. Rope and wheels can be clearly seen above, as can the implications of the counter-balanced mineral traffic which used it. As empty wagons descended, trucks laden with coal for Tresavean's mines ascended. Time taken was 7–8 minutes, and a customary load of four 12 ton trucks of coal was well within the maximum permissible pull of 84 tons gross. In later years coal traffic declined, and tin took its place. Later still, a desultory trade in grain, fertilisers etc guaranteed ultimate closure of the branch on 1 January 1936.

Meanwhile, railway history was also being made elsewhere in Cornwall. In September 1844 a newly formed company, the West Cornwall Railway, expressed the firm intention of linking Truro to Penzance by rail. The line was to be leased and worked by Hayle Railway, and the Truro-Penzance section was to be operated on the atmospheric system. Alas, Parliament considered the inclines at Penponds and Angarrack too dangerous for regular passenger traffic. Thus, the Bill was rejected. Back came a new Bill, incorporating deviations which would avoid the two inclines, and proposing West Cornwall purchase, with GWR support, of Hayle Railway. This one succeeded, and received Royal Assent on 3 August 1846. In the controversy which followed, WCR were given permission to lay single standard-gauge track, 'with layout wide enough to permit broad-gauge track to be laid, in accordance with the terms of the original Act'. Now it was clear why the Great Western were interested!

Time passed, and when Penzance Station, a 'commodious structure of wood', according to local reports, was first inspected by the chairman and directors of West Cornwall Railway in February 1852, it was all done very quietly. Seven months later, however, by which time WCR had succeeded in completing its route, and opening day arrived, public temperature had soared; so much so that the first through train from Truro to Penzance not only required 32 coaches and *three* engines, but its arrival was greeted by thousands of wildly cheering Cornish citizens! The day, 25 August, had even been set aside as a public holiday. Later, under sustained pressure from the GWR, dual gauge tracks for goods and passenger services evolved; and, on 1 March 1867, history was made on an even grander scale, when the first through train from Paddington entered Penzance Station.

28 August 1936: In this view, Penzance Station, with its distinctive wooden roof, has hardly altered since broad-gauge trains frequented it seventy years earlier. Even the advertisement for Opie's Family & Commercial Hotel ('Turn left top of Main Street') adds a whiff of bygone innocence with its blandishments: 'Baths Free. Billiards played on Sundays. Commercial & Special. Lower Weekends. GARAGE'. Today, fifty years on, advertising may be more sophisticated—but the GWR's old station, its platforms lengthened in 1938–39, still serves British Rail.

The sleek-looking chocolate and cream liveried coaches standing at the

28 August 1936 (3)

platform, bearing new headboards, 'Cornish Riviera Limited', offer an interesting evocation of GWR centenary events in 1935. First GWR coaches to have large compartment windows, two of these brand new ten-coach sets were made available for 'Cornish Riviera' service in July 1935. The streamlined *King Henry VII* was even photographed, for publicity purposes, at the head of one of the sets. Rather sadly, the new 'Centenary' stock was transferred elsewhere in 1941, for wartime reasons—and ended its post-war existence on rather less glamorous service.

Somewhere on his way home—for once his notebook does not specify an exact location—Le Manquais, vigilant as ever, did not allow another example of GWR enterprise to pass unnoticed.

29 August 1936

29 August 1936: In addition to displaying the rather less flamboyant circular totem that GWR chose to adopt in 1934, No 5032 *Usk Castle*, one of ten 'Castles' added that year, carries an experimental eight-wheeled tender which was built at Swindon in 1931. The only one of its kind, it weighed 49 tons 3 cwt when fully loaded; 2½ tons heavier than the enlarged 4,000-gallon six-wheeled tender previously introduced. Switched around quite freely, this unique tender was associated with seven other 'Castles', four 'Halls', and a 'Star' during its lifetime. But a second was never built.

At Easter 1937 the GWR's publicly advertised intention to run a Good Friday 'Ramblers' Excursion' from Paddington to Winchester caught Le Manquais' imagination. Besides, it offered him a splendid excuse to embark on another year's photography. He duly reported to Paddington, and was so intrigued to find that an elderly 'Duke' was to handle the excursion throughout that he got his camera out on the spot.

26 March 1937 (1)

26 March 1937: Despite her 37 years, No 3283 *Comet* looks in sprightly form as she awaits the right of way at Paddington. One of sixty 'Duke' Class built at Swindon to William Dean's order in 1895–99, *Comet* was given the privilege of receiving the first of the GWR's new standard type Belpaire boilers in 1903. Originally numbered 3315, the engine was renumbered 3283 until 1946, when all eleven surviving 'Dukes' had their first two digits altered to '90' to make room for newly built 0–6–0s. Thus, *Comet* acquired a third number, 9083, and perished as such, second last of her class, at BR hands in December 1950. She had completed well over one million miles.

Built to tackle heavy main line gradients in Devon and Cornwall, the

'Dukes' commanded all important trains betwen Exeter and Penzance until
the turn of the century; when, first, 'Bulldogs', then Churchward 2–6–0s,
superseded them. After Grouping many enjoyed a new lease of life on the
Cambrian main line; and by 1930 six were also stationed at Didcot for use
on the Winchester line. Hence, *Comet* was about to run on familiar metals
this Good Friday morning.

26 March 1937 (2)

26 March 1937: A brief stop *en route* at Newbury allows time to capture ex-
Cambrian Railways' 0–6–0 No 908 as it simmered opposite on a train bound
for Lambourn; another branch service which was to disappear in the 1960s.
The clerestory-roofed coach lying next to the engine adds conviction to a
vintage scene. Fitted soon after grouping with a standard GWR '2021' Class
Belpaire boiler, No 908's appearance, in fact, belies her age. Built in 1873 by
Sharp Stewart & Co (Works No 2339) for Mid-Wales Railway, the engine
passed into Cambrian Railways' ownership in April 1888, and was one of
nine such 0–6–0s taken over by the GWR in May 1922. It was as well,
though, that Le Manquais photographed her, for No 908 was withdrawn in
December 1938.

Once the Special reached Winchester, it transpired, rather amusingly, that Le
Manquais had his own ideas on the subject of 'rambling'. Pausing only long enough
to photograph Winchester (Chesil) Station, and follow *Comet* round to Winchester's
modest engine shed, he then switched to ex-L&SWR metals and enjoyed a day at
Southampton Docks! By the time he found his way back to Chesil, *Comet* was back at
the head of the 'Ramblers' Excursion', ready as ever for the run home. Next day Le
Manquais was back down south, at Headcorn Junction, ready to enjoy a splendid day
on the Kent & East Sussex Light Railway. His main holiday that year, a fortnight in
Northern Ireland, followed in June and subsequent brief trips concentrated chiefly
on Metropolitan and Southern Railway locations.

1938 looked a more promising year from a GWR point of view. Short trips to Liverpool, Hereford, Wrexham, Shrewsbury, and Welshpool, however, produced no great evidence of GWR involvement. Then he turned towards the Severn Valley.

18 April 1938

18 April 1938: Heading for Bridgnorth and points south, GWR 2–6–2T No 5527 and train pause at Ironbridge & Broseley Station. From the platform here one could obtain an excellent view of Ironbridge Gorge. Not far away lay Coalbrookdale where Richard Trevithick built his first steam engine, a commercial failure, in 1802. A second local phase of locomotive building, however, during the Railway Mania produced six 0–4–0STs during 1864–66. One of them, No 5, has been a key exhibit in the Coalbrookdale Museum of Iron at Ironbridge since 1959. GWR Shrewsbury-Bridgnorth metals, alas, were lifted in 1963. The 2–6–2 tank, first introduced by Churchward in 1903, had long been a favourite with GWR men and No 5527 was one of 155 '4500' Class locos added between 1906 and 1929. They were really a replica of the '4400' series built earlier, except that an increase in coupled wheel diameter to 4ft 7½in greatly enhanced speed, and their ability to handle a wide range of duties. As a consequence these nippy little tanks could be found on branch service all over the West Country. The iron struts between smokebox and front buffer beam were introduced in 1909 to relieve strain on the frames. All 155 '4500' Class tanks survived to enter BR stock, and No 5527 was not withdrawn until June 1960.

Sadly, the year 1938 was to finish in disaster as far as the GWR was concerned. I shall never know what brought Le Manquais to Paddington Station on the morning of Saturday, 26 November; but, significantly, the first photograph he took was one of the burned-out shell of Paddington Arrival signal cabin. But I am convinced the act was not one of voyeurism on his part. He was too deeply, almost professionally, involved in railway signalling to feel other than great sympathy for Paddington's predicament.

26 November 1938

26 November 1938: A sad sight some thirty hours after Paddington's disastrous fire. About 2.00 am on the morning of 25 November smoke and flames were seen to be issuing from Paddington Arrival Signalbox. LCC Fire brigades attended promptly enough, but the greater part of the electrical installation was destroyed. As communications between Edgware Road and Paddington and Paddington and Westbourne Park were completely disrupted, drastic and speedy measures had to be adopted. Up trains were immediately time interval-worked, and points were worked by hand. Even Paddington Departure Box was affected. Use of the Hammersmith & City Line was also severely affected, and local trains were terminated at Westbourne Park. Some outer suburban services had to be withdrawn temporarily; though Ealing trains were allowed into Paddington after 7.00 am, under caution. GWR staff must have worked like Trojans that day. Temporary block instruments installed between Paddington Arrival and the next box, Subway Junction, were brought into use at 5.00 pm, and this made accelerated acceptance of main line trains possible.

By now the true extent of the disaster could be assessed. The burned out box had contained the equivalent of 209 working levers. London Passenger Transport Board assisted early by offering three side frames; and these were rapidly converted into a whole frame of 141 levers. Eighteen days after the fire a temporary signal box, installed initially for suburban services only, began to handle main line services as well, and gradually Paddington groped its way back to normal. But 50 miles of wire alone were required in subsequent repairs.

One month later, amidst quite an active spell of photography over the Christmas period, Le Manquais was able to verify to his own satisfaction that GWR had surmounted their problems.

27 December 1938

27 December 1938: Pause for reflection, in more ways than one, as snow on Didcot Station platforms begins to melt, and the 10.45 am ex-Paddington makes a stately entrance with No 5070 *Sir Daniel Gooch* at its head. Original intention was to name this 'Castle', shopped in June 1938, *Bridgwater Castle*. At an Annual General Meeting of GWR shareholders held in February 1938, however, the decision was made to revive the revered names of Brunel and Gooch after a lapse of eight years. Former broad-gauge and standard-gauge locos had previously carried the names since 1865. Thus, two men who had served the GWR so illustriously—Brunel as Civil Engineer from 1833 to 1859, and Gooch as the GWR's first Locomotive Superintendent (1837–64), then Chairman (1865–89)—were once again honoured in the milieu they had striven so hard to create.

I am sure Le Manquais must have felt his photograph made an appropriate ending to a momentous GWR year.

CHAPTER SIX

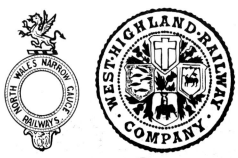

WALES and SCOTLAND

According to his notebooks, Frederick Le Manquais' initial descent upon Wales landed him fair and square at Dinas Junction. It would be interesting to know how he got there, but the real significance of his journey to such a remote spot is of even greater interest. For Dinas, as it happened, was also the northern extremity of the Welsh Highland Railway, and the year 1934 was a critical one in the affairs of that extremely frail concern.

Only eleven years old in its present form, though it had precedents dating back to 1877, the WHR had long stumbled its over-optimistic way against heavy odds. Now, however, the net was tightening. Weary of financial uncertainty and already saddled with worthless WHR Debentures, local authorities had had enough and, with the sole dissention of Portmadoc UDC, were urging that the 1ft 11½in gauge line should be closed forthwith. Pressure continued to mount. Early in 1934 both the LMSR and the GWR politely, but firmly, declined invitations to work the ailing concern, and only rather desperate latterday negotiations with Festiniog Railway enabled WHR passenger services to be resumed in the summer of 1934. Terms were tough. The WHR was leased to Festiniog from 1 July at a nominal rent of £1 for the first six months, and a proportion of traffic receipts thereafter.

No doubt the fact that Colonel H. F. Stephens had, in the past, been intimately associated with both Festiniog and the WHR stimulated Le Manquais' interest wonderfully. Certainly, no sooner had he arrived at Dinas Junction than he was out, camera at the ready, photographing *Russell*, one-time pride of North Wales Narrow Gauge Railways, the Welsh Highland's immediate predecessor. Alas, for once in his life our photographer contrived to execute a double exposure ('Dud', his notebook remarks laconically), and we have to bear with him all the way south to Bedgellert to see what ensued.

11 August 1934: All change at Bedgellert, and WHR 4-6-0T No 590

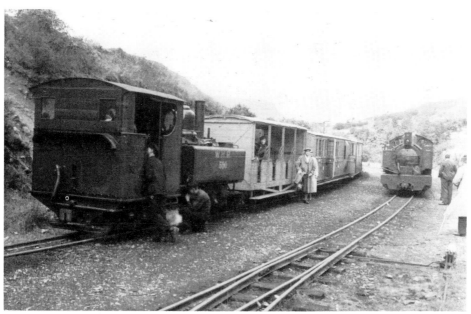

11 August 1934 (1)

(Baldwin No 45172/1917), bought for £240 in July 1923, looks sprightly enough as it waits to leave for Portmadoc with its multi-coloured train. The latter was one of several ideas only just introduced in an effort to brighten the WHR's public image. On the right, meanwhile, 2–6–2T No 12 *Russell*, not deigning to tread on Festiniog metals, rests after bringing in its Dinas connection. Her crew, nevertheless, have drifted across for a chat. Festiniog management, implementing their lease over the WHR's ailing affairs, were running a summer service of four passenger trains daily between Portmadoc and Bedgellert, with five in the reverse direction. Festiniog locomotives never ran on Welsh Highland's northern metals, thus, at Bedgellert a reduced service by WHR stock conveyed passengers to and from Dinas Junction. Latterly even that brave effort proved to be of no avail, and WHR passenger services finally tottered to a standstill on 26 September 1936.

The thirty-seater 'Toastrack' car seen next to No 590 was one of six War Department-design bogie carriages, built by Robert Hudson Ltd of Leeds, which were purchased by Festiniog in July 1923. Numbered 37–42, working life for most was comparatively short. Four of them, Nos 38–41, were converted to flat wagons in 1926–28. Nos 37 and 42, both lying derelict by 1929, were later restored to service, and remained so until Festiniog passenger services ceased in 1939. Ultimately the two surviving 'Hudsons' were stripped of their upper works, and, from 1953 onwards, were employed as flat wagon and weed-killer vehicle respectively.

11 August 1934: This view of Welsh Highland metals, taken looking south from Bedgellert, illustrates only too clearly the kind of journey Le Manquais could anticipate before he reached Portmadoc. Three years later, when all traffic ceased on WHR, *Russell* was allotted the melancholy task of running

11 August 1934 (2)

between Bedgellert and Portmadoc to salvage the Baldwin tank and such wagons as lay abandoned *en route*. Thence the two locos, eight passenger coaches, and 104 wagons lay idle at Dinas, until the Ministry of Supply requisitioned the lot in 1941. Track was lifted to speed the war effort, carriages were auctioned, and the Baldwin tank was cut up on the spot. Only *Russell* and the remains of *Moel Tryfan* survived, and the former, after several subsequent Houdini-like escapes, may yet again rouse echoes on former Welsh Highland Railway territory.

Historically, through passenger service between Dinas and Portmadoc only became feasible on 1 June 1923, the opening date of the Welsh Highland Railway and the latter's method of establishing a firm presence at Portmadoc was both interesting and ingenious. It built a station called Portmadoc (New) immediately south of the

GWR's Cambrian main line, and gained access thereto by introducing a level crossing over the GWR line. Thence narrow-gauge metals carried on from New Station into Portmadoc Harbour. The Festiniog, no doubt with the blessing of its Civil Engineer and Locomotive Superintendent, Col H. F. Stephens, co-operated by building a new linking line through Portmadoc streets. Thereafter nearly all Festiniog trains ran to and from Portmadoc (New) Station.

Four years later, when a receiver was appointed to a moribund WHR, Stephens demonstrated that he had not lost his touch. Exercising his well known flair for light railway economies, he had a small halt built at Portmadoc, immediately *north* of the GWR crossing. From then on passengers from Dinas and Bedgellert had no option but to alight at this halt, and cross GWR metals by foot, shepherded by the guard, to reach Portmadoc (New), where Festiniog trains provided a shuttle service to and from Portmadoc Harbour. Aware that the purpose of this tactical manoeuvre lay in sparing the WHR from making payments of over £150 per year to the GWR, towards maintaining and manning the level crossing, Le Manquais must have smiled to himself as he alighted at Stephen's northern halt!

11 August 1934 (3)

11 August 1934: Still *in situ*, and long the subject of controversy between WHR and GWR, though not used for years, WHR's level crossing with GWR metals north of Portmadoc was made of cast manganese steel. The rather primitive halt Stephens introduced lies behind the white gates in the background. Though all Welsh Highland traffic ceased on 19 June 1937, the WHR crossing was not taken out until 1938, on which occasion the signalbox was also removed. The single-track main line in the foreground, formerly the property of Cambrian Railways, ran (left to right) between Pwllheli and Aberystwyth.

11 August 1934 (4)

11 August 1934: A last look at No 590 as, now running boiler-first, it pre-
pares to leave Portmadoc halt on its return journey to Bedgellert. Baldwin
Locomotive Works built hundreds of these little American 4–6–0Ts during
World War 1 for service behind the Allied Lines, and, originally 60cm in
gauge, a number of them were exposed for sale by the British Ministry of
Munitions around 1921. Glyn Valley bought one, as did the Welsh Highland, and Ashover Light Railway, advised by Colonel Stephens, acquired *six*.
Never too popular with British locomen, the Baldwins rode roughly, and
tended to be such unreliable steamers that most were usually confined to
freight duties. Though painted red by this time, as opposed to its earlier
funereal black, No 590's appearance here on passenger duties was a clear indication of the WHR's straitened financial circumstances.

But did any light railway thrive in the harsh climate of the late 1920s and early
1930s? What with general trade depression and merciless road competition the
Festiniog Railway itself was gradually being squeezed to a shadow of its former self.
Such, indeed, were its difficulties that from 1930 Festiniog's 'full' summer passenger
service had shrunk to four daily trains each way. Winter passenger service confined
itself to a morning and evening train for a steadily decreasing population of quarry-
men. Sad times for a proud Welsh concern which, a century earlier, had been the first
to convince authority that passengers could safely be conveyed over metals narrower
than standard-gauge! Even Colonel Stephens' association with the Festiniog from
1923 onwards had been something of a mixed blessing for, while his enterprise and
enthusiasm undoubtedly postponed the evil day, his insistence on controlling the
Welsh railway largely by the issue of military-like memos from his 'Head Office' in
Tonbridge deeply offended Festiniog men. Thus, any time Stephens chose to pay a

visit of inspection to Boston Lodge Works etc, news of his arrival soon spread down the line, and every artifice was brought to bear in attempts to bamboozle him. They rarely succeeded, of course—but neither was the Colonel amused . . !

Ah, well, poor Stephens had departed this life by the time Le Manquais visited Portmadoc Harbour Station. But the deep melancholy of Festiniog affairs was plain to be seen; for the place had a desolate air about it. Double Fairlie *Taliesin* was just in the act of leaving as Le Manquais arrived, and the best he could do was to capture sister engine *Merddin Emrys* as it stood by in Portmadoc yard.

11 August 1934 (5)

11 August 1934: A living, and logical, conclusion to Robert Fairlie's aversion to turntables and locomotive tenders, double Fairlie No 10 *Merddin Emrys*, home-built in 1879 by Festiniog Railway, was Boston Lodge's first locomotive product. Placed in traffic in July that year, it was subsequently reboilered in 1896 and 1921. Heavy boiler and firebox repairs were also effected by Avonside Engine Company in 1934, whence the little engine served Festiniog faithfully until all traffic ceased on 1 August 1946. Later came Festiniog's miraculous resurrection in July 1955—and a passenger train again travelled between Portmadoc and Boston Lodge. The rest is modern railway history: *Merddin Emrys*, extensively repaired, appeared again on 21 April 1961, although the cab roof seen in this 1934 picture was not replaced and two weatherboards sufficed to protect the crew. A new tapered chimney was also fitted in place of that seen here. Reboilered eight years later, it resumed normal operations. But Festiniog locomotive technique was also advancing rapidly, and, late in 1972, *Merddin Emrys* became the last active Festiniog locomotive to be converted to oil burning.

11 August 1934: Also seen by Le Manquais at Portmadoc was this engaging

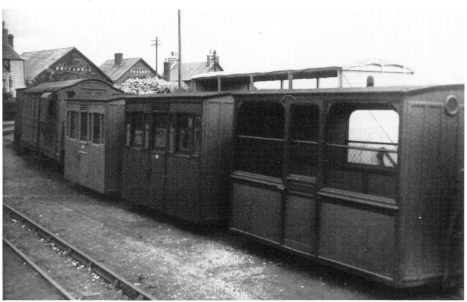

11 August 1934 (6)

collection of vintage Festiniog Railway four-wheeled carriages. All were built by Brown Marshall & Company between 1864 and 1867. Observation coach No 12, nearest the camera, was originally completely open, with tarpaulin roof and sides. Fourteen third class passengers were somehow packed along its knifeboard seating. It was rebuilt in the form seen above during the early 1930s, and wire safety screens were fitted as a safety precaution. The original waist-high panels of companion coaches, Nos 4 and 5, have also been replaced by boarded sides, and four small windows have taken the place of earlier wooden panelling. By this time, too, vacuum brake piping had been fitted. No 12 was scrapped in 1958, but Nos 4 and 5 still survive. The taller coach roof seen behind belongs, of course, to the second surviving Hudson 'Toastrack'.

Almost four years later Le Manquais, not content with investigating Shropshire & Montgomeryshire Light Railway metals, crowned a remarkable day's activity by conducting a similar inspection of Welshpool & Llanfair Light Railway's base at Welshpool Station yard. Like the Festiniog, this 2ft 6in gauge Welsh railway had seen better days. From the time it was opened in 1903 Cambrian Railways worked the 9½-mile line with two Beyer Peacock 0–6–0Ts. At Grouping the W&LLR passed into GWR ownership but the little railway was kept going for a number of years, even in the teeth of severe bus competition, until the GWR, finally wearying of it all, brought passenger services to a close in February 1931. A minimal freight service continued to function, however, and therefore W&LLR's modest Welshpool establishment, with its carriage and loco shed, was still alive, though only just, when Le Manquais paid his respects to a deserted station yard that Saturday afternoon.

16 April 1938: Though regular passenger services on the Welshpool & Llanfair Light Railway were terminated by GWR on 9 February 1931, one

16 April 1938

return freight train still ran daily between the two small towns: hence this weekend view of 2ft 6in and standard gauge stock awaiting attention at Welshpool's Transhipment Shed. The narrow-gauge metals which connected the two establishments can be seen crossing in the foreground.

'Break of gauge', with its additional expense, always had little appeal for main line companies engaged in keenly competitive freight traffic. Indeed, one GWR manager, in giving evidence before the Allport Commission of 1887, was frank enough to testify that Paddington, in dealing with such circumstances, automatically added twenty miles' rates to cover the costs of transhipment. Nevertheless, the practice persisted at Welshpool until BR withdrew narrow-gauge rail services in November 1956.

Fortunately, the Welshpool & Llanfair saga finished, like those of other Welsh narrow-gauge railways, on a happy note. Fostered by enthusiasts, it resumed operations, still employing its two Beyer Peacock tanks, from Castle Caereinion in 1963, and it has since forged 4¼ miles eastward towards a brand new station at Raven Square, on the outskirts of Welshpool.

Three years prior to his Welshpool visit, in April 1935, Le Manquais made his first visit to Scotland. Strangely, it was only a weekend visit; and, as no evidence exists to the contrary, we may safely assume that he travelled overnight from King's Cross. Certainly, he left the train at Newcastle Central next morning, for High Level Bridge and its adjacent Swing Bridge were the first objects to attract his camera. Equally surely, he spent the remainder of that Friday at Berwick, where still more bridges and that lovely gentle old town quite captured his imagination. One can well appreciate his excitement as his train swung through Tweedmouth station, and suddenly revealed that wonderfully dramatic view of the Tweed estuary. No matter what the Border sign a mile or two further north was about to say, once he crossed that graceful viaduct he was well and truly in *North British* Railway territory. The fact that the insignia of that railway flaunted the arms of both Edinburgh and Berwick was no accident.

19 April 1935

19 April 1935: Nearly, but not quite, in Scotland, Le Manquais pauses by the side of the River Tweed to admire Berwick's Royal Border Bridge. An ex-NER 4–4–0 is crossing from Tweedmouth shed, probably to take up passenger duties on the Berwick-St Boswells branch. At 2,160ft long, 126ft high, and embodying 28 61½ft arches, the famous viaduct, opened by Queen Victoria on 29 August 1850, and built by Robert Stephenson, provided a last eagerly awaited link in what was to become the LNER's East Coast route between Edinburgh and London. To celebrate the official opening NBR painted Crampton engine No 55 in Royal Stewart tartan livery(!) for the purpose of hauling a Royal train on to Edinburgh. Mercifully, by all accounts, elaborate decorations hung additionally about the engine and tender tended to soften the somewhat bizarre effect.

We might pause, also, at this juncture to reflect on the imminent expectations of a railway enthusiast who was weaned on Southern Railway activity. There can be little doubt that the variety of engines Le Manquais would soon be seeing would stimulate someone already well used to SR's engaging 'mix' of L&SWR, SE&CR, and London Brighton motive power. So, too, would the recurring Dugald Drummond theme which was so long and earnestly cultivated by the Caledonian, North British, and Highland Railways alike.

Consider, too, the locomotive sheds he was about to witness during his brief weekend in Scotland. Tweedmouth offered a last NER shed, with possibly an NBR engine or two about to whet the appetite. Next came Dunbar, whose small shed held only a pilot engine. Then, as his train entered Edinburgh, St Margarets shed would loom up, both left and right, the latter a modest roundhouse sheltering Leith Dock 'pugs', the former, the main shed, proferring a bustling passing view of NB passenger locos, including, if he were fortunate, a first glimpse of NBR's mighty green 'Atlantics'.

Rather surprisingly, Le Manquais, impressed though he must have been by Waverley Station, did not choose to dally in Edinburgh. He was heading for Perth, and, again in the absence of specific information, my guess is that he walked along Princes Street gardens, and resumed his journey from the Caledonian Railway's old station at Princes Street. Even so, he would still have a fine view of the LNER's Haymarket shed, with its intriguing blend of NB engines, NER 'Atlantics', and Gresley 'Pacifics', as his train swung in to join LNER metals to Polmont. Then, once past Falkirk Grahamston station, his LMS train would veer north for Larbert. It was there that he obtained his first photographic reminder that cheek by jowl operations by LNER and LMSR were quite commonplace in this area.

20 April 1935

20 April 1935: Though it was an LMSR station, Larbert was quite used to entertaining LNER locomotives. Indeed, the whole of Central Scotland was a positive maze of mutual running powers between the two major companies. In this view, No 2920, Doncaster-built in 1931, and one of nearly fifty 'V1' 2-6-2Ts allocated to the Scottish Area during the 1930s, waits with its mixed stopping passenger train of NBR and LNER coaches before setting out for Edinburgh (Waverley). It will employ the same route to Haymarket as did Le Manquais' LMS train from Edinburgh (Princes Street).

A year or two earlier, before the 'V1s' arrived, an ex-NBR 'D31' 4–4–0 would have handled this train.

Soon Le Manquais was deep in former Caledonian Railway territory and I like to imagine the pleasure and excitement he must have felt when, some ten miles further on, the LMSR shed, just south of Stirling station, floated past his eyes. Were he in luck he may well have noted an ex-CR 'Oban Bogie' 4–6–0 amongst its inmates; for a handful of these sturdy old McIntosh veterans had still not yielded up their birthright. Further north, the run in towards Perth General Station offered even greater delights. The old Caley shed, now known as Perth (South), would be quite full on a Saturday afternoon, and Le Manquais may even have had his first glimpse of the CR's famous single-wheeler, now LMS No 14010, for the engine was still working between Perth and Dundee. In any case, no doubt he made the locomotive's acquaintance in later years, when, beautifully restored in Caledonian blue, it travelled the length and breadth of the UK as No 123. Meanwhile, dreams over Perth (South) shed's contents were hardly in order, for, almost immediately, before entering Perth General station, a smaller LNER shed put in an appearance. Again if fortune favoured him, our traveller may have spotted a green ex-NBR 'Atlantic' lounging outside; for a brace of St Margarets beauties were still working the Edinburgh-Perth route at this time. One such was 9904 *Holyrood*.

According to this notebooks Le Manquais only paused at Perth long enough to photograph his first Highland Railway engine, No 14392 *Loch Naver*. His return south was certainly part of a hurried schedule, for later that day he photographed MacBrayne's 'diesel-electric ship' *Loch Fyne* as it lay alongside its berth in Glasgow! Next morning his camera was out at Carlisle Station, recording (unnamed) 'Jubilee' No 5625 as it backed onto his southbound train. His brief Scottish introduction was over.

Over it may have been, but its impact was so momentous that he embarked on a full fortnight's holiday in Scotland the following year. This time he really meant business and, again, he must have travelled up overnight—for the first indication we have that he was up in Scotland is a typically unusual Le Manquais view of the Forth Bridge. *Now* where was he off to?

> *7 June 1936*: An interesting Sunday morning aspect of the Forth Bridge, as seen from North Queensferry's neat, but deserted, platforms. Nearly on the bridge itself, what appears to be a maintenance train awaits permission to switch over to the southbound line, and at sea level, a little further right, a ferry can just be discerned making its way out from South Queensferry's foreshore. Built to the design of Sir John Fowler and Sir Benjamin Baker, with Sir William Arrol as contractor, Scotland's great 8,298ft long railway bridge was opened by the Prince of Wales, later King Edward VII, on 4 March 1890. Its two main 1,710ft spans afford a clearance of 157ft above the Forth at high water.
>
> A joint undertaking by four major railway companies—NBR, NER, GNR and MR—as far back as 1873, the huge bridge took eight years to build; and its completion enabled NBR to score heavily over its arch-rival,

the Caledonian, in that distances from Edinburgh to Aberdeen were now:
NBR 130 miles, CR 159 miles—a reversal of the previous pecking order.

7 June 1936 (1)

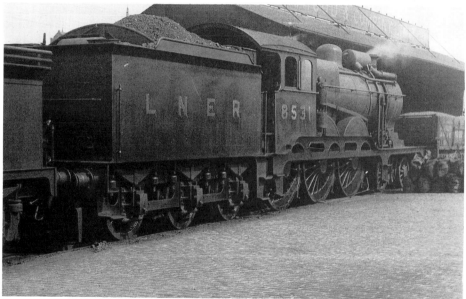

7 June 1936 (2)

7 June 1936: No doubt Le Manquais was well aware that eleven ex-GER
Class 'B12' 4–6–0s had been transferred to the LNER's GNS Section during
1931–33, but he hardly could have known that individual 'B12s' quite often
found their way to Dundee, Glasgow and Edinburgh. One presumes, therefore, that he must have been agreeably surprised to find No 8531 standing
outside Dundee (Tay Bridge) shed as to the manner born. The ACFI feed-
water heating apparatus, still born aloft the boiler, was possibly one reason

why the 'B12s' were known to Scottish locomen as 'Hikers'. Once the GNSR men mastered new driving and firing techniques, however, the 'B12s' performed very creditably in the north of Scotland, and were not superseded until Thompson 'B1s' arrived in 1947. No 8531 temporarily returned to South Western England during 1944–46, on ambulance train duties. Its eventual return to Scotland was, alas, marred by comparatively early withdrawal in November 1947.

Clearly Le Manquais did not linger long at Dundee, for the passage of little more than twenty-four hours found this astonishing man on the west coast of Scotland—admiring the shipping at Gourock, Dunoon, and Rothesay! Next day, by courtesy of NBR's West Highland route and that of the CR to Oban, he alighted at Connel Ferry, where both station and bridge occupied his camera. So, too, did the beauties of Loch Etive.

9 June 1936

9 June 1936: Highland weather and the gradient board tell their own stories as ex-HR 4-6-0 No 14686 *Urquart Castle* enters Tyndrum station on its Oban-Stirling train. In contrast to the famous 'Rivers' episode (see p. 128) this was a time when LMSR found ex-Highland Railway express engines eminently suitable for West Highland work over Caledonian metals. Here, too, at Tyndrum the former Callander & Oban railway route, opened in 1880, marched alongside NBR's West Highland line, vintage 1894, for five miles to Crianlarich, before pressing on east to Killin Junction. A fascinating variety of locomotives trod both metals in their time, but by early BR days Stanier 'Black Fives' had taken fair command in both sectors.

From Tyndrum our traveller pressed north, and further west, back again on LNER metals. Somewhere around Lochailort we discover that his West Highland train was hauled by ex-GNR 'K2' 2–6–0 No 4652 and one of NBR's ubiquitous 'Glens', No 9406 *Glen Croe*. Mallaig, his ultimate destination, was not far away.

10 June 1936

10 June 1936: Quite possibly, but for Grouping in 1923, the North British Railway would have introduced an eight-coupled mineral locomotive. As it was, it contented itself with Class 'S', a final, and excellent, superheated development of the classic 0–6–0 wheel arrangement. A total of 104 were built between 1914 and 1921. They were reclassified 'J37' by LNER, and no engines served their masters better. Such was their versatility, all continued in BR harness to the bitter end of steam. In LNER days they could be found all over the Scottish region, hence this picture of No 9303, complete with express headlamps, heading a Fort William train at Mallaig station. An NB Locomotive Co product of January 1920, No 9303 continued to serve until December 1962. February 1966 saw the class extinct.

Presumably Le Manquais took that Fort William train; for the next morning found him on the shores of Loch Linnhe.

11 June 1936: Favourite NBR passenger engines on the West Highland line were, undoubtedly, the 'Glens', built at Cowlairs in 1913–20, and classified 'D34' by the LNER. For more than twenty years these hardy 4–4–0s took the lion's share of West Highland traffic, and throughout LNER days more than half the class could always be found at Glasgow's Eastfield shed. Thus, No 9408 *Glen Sloy* presented a more than familiar silhouette as it

11 June 1936 (1)

posed at Banavie Pier for this photograph. This very modest branch left the main line at Banavie Junction, one mile west of Fort William, and ran 1¾ miles to Banavie Pier Station, which was situated on the Caledonian Canal. It saw its first train on 1 June 1895. NBR hopes, however, that traffic on the branch might justify a further thrust towards Inverness were never realized—and the Banavie branch closed on 2 September 1939.

Determined to make the most of what was very likely a 'Freedom of Scotland' ticket, Le Manquais could not resist moving on to Fort Augustus, another child of sorrow as far as NBR was concerned. Joining the West Highland line at Spean Bridge, the Invergarry & Fort Augustus Railway, opened on 22 July 1903, was first worked by the Highland Railway. Somewhat disillusioned, the Highland moved out nearly four years later, and NBR, no doubt visualizing eventual extension to Inverness, worked the line as a West Highland branch from 1 May 1907. Once again, realization fell far short of ambition. Service on the 24-mile branch line was suspended on 31 October 1911, and, although reopened on 1 August 1913 after the NBR purchased the concern for £27,000, it had little to offer the LNER when Grouping arrived. Eventually passenger traffic on the branch ended on 30 November 1933. One coal train continued to run on Saturdays, then all traffic ceased on 1 January 1947 and the track was dismantled. Presumably Le Manquais bussed to Fort Augustus in the year 1936.

11 June 1936: Sad times at Fort Augustus, a community now served only by one weekly coal train. The presence of a motor car suggests that someone still lived in the station house but, that apart, platforms and station buildings are deserted, and at the northern end of the island platform a barrier is placed across the track where Highland Railway trains once conveyed passengers on to Pier station, whence they found themselves on the very shore of Loch Ness. Rail service to Pier station was suspended a long time prior to this picture, in September 1906, and it was never resumed once the NBR

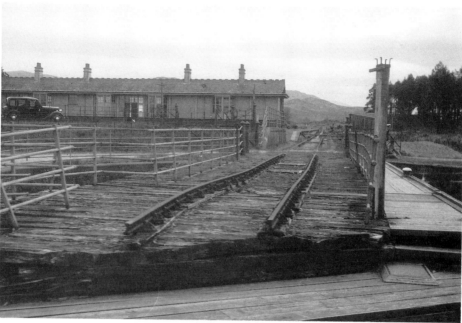

11 June 1936 (2)

took over the following year. Soon the line fell into decay, and the NBR hastened the process by demolishing Pier station's modest building. The hand-operated swing bridge which permitted trains to cross the Caledonian Canal was left permanently open to allow free passage of ships. It was left to the LNER to complete the sad process nearly twelve years after this photograph was taken, when the Spean Bridge-Fort Augustus branch closed to all traffic on 1 January 1947. The last trace of railway track at Fort Augustus soon disappeared.

Despite the absence of the rail link that the NBR always aspired to create, Le Manquais somehow found his way further north to Inverness. Then, launching himself enthusiastically into Highland Railway territory, he aimed for Dingwall.

12 June 1936: The distinct sea change which overtook LMSR locomotive affairs in the Highland Section right through the 1930s is exemplified by this dramatic study of Stanier 'Black Five' No 5159 as it paused at Dingwall with its Kyle train. Initially ten 'Crab' 2-6-0s were sent up from the south and they adapted themselves very happily to Highland conditions. A few years later, however, an influx of Stanier's new '5MTs', with their ubiquitous versatility, soon gained dominance all over Northern Scotland; and held it right to the dying days of steam.

In 1936 an early morning train from Inverness to the north, and an afternoon service which connected with a ship plying between Scrabster Harbour (Thurso) and the Orkneys, was named the 'Orcadian'. Three years earlier, trains to and from Kyle of Lochalsh connecting with Mac Brayne ships had been given the names 'Hebridean' and 'Lewisman'.

12 June 1936

12 June 1936: Long famous as a Spa, the small town of Strathpeffer lay at the end of a four-mile branch from Dingwall, and here ex-CR 0–4–4T No 15199, St Rollox-built in 1909, is following time-honoured tradition as it leads in its ex-HR coach and miscellany of goods vehicles. Rather incongruously, a goods van brings up the rear. The ornate platform canopy, meanwhile, reflects the importance of Strathpeffer's passenger traffic. The station itself opened on 3 June 1885, and once the HR invested in a hotel there in

July 1911 a 'Strathpeffer Express' ran additionally, on Tuesdays only, from Aviemore. Curiously, there was no return train! This odd service, however, was withdrawn during World War 1, and was never restored. Ultimately, all passenger service was withdrawn by the LMSR on 23 February 1946. Later, under BR auspices, freight traffic, too, ceased from 26 March 1951, and the branch line was dismantled. The Caley tank was found other employment, and lasted until July 1961.

Having passed the first week of his holiday in exciting new circumstances, Le Manquais now paused at Inverness to consider which route he would choose to take him back to London. Eventually, rather intriguingly, he elected to sample eastbound metals which once took the Highland Railway as far as Keith.

16 June 1936

16 June 1936: At Forres, halfway between Inverness and Keith, a real surprise lay in wait, in the shape of ex-HR 4–4–0 No 14380 *Loch Ness*, still shining bright in immediate post-Grouping LMSR maroon livery. The engine even carried MR-type smokebox number plates, a decoration many HR and CR engines disdained to flaunt. The distinctive HR cab, with its Stroudleyesque roof, was destined to serve the engine for the rest of its days, but gone was the louvred chimney it bore when it left Dubs & Co's works in 1896. David Jones' last design before his enforced retirement that year, eighteen of these handsome locos served HR well. Fifteen were built in 1896, and, rather surprisingly, three more of this proven design were added by Christopher Cumming in 1916. One of ten fitted later with ex-CR boilers, *Loch Ness* perished at LMSR hands in December 1940.

By 18 June even Le Manquais knew it was time to turn south. As our final three pictures show, however, he still allowed himself a pleasurable leisurely schedule.

18 June 1936 (1)

18 June 1936: In this charming scene at Pitlochry station ex-CR 0–6–0 No 17454, one of the legendary 'Jumbos', is entering with its Struan-Perth stopping train. The two ladies in the foreground seem well inured to the spectacle of station porter and fireman changing single-line tokens. Though only classified '2F' by LMSR, the first of these evergreen Drummond locomotives, maids of all work, emerged from both St Rollox and Neilson & Co's Works in November 1883. Perpetuated later by Drummond's successors, the class eventually increased to 244 engines. Many were fitted with Westinghouse brake to work passenger trains, and, quite remarkably, the whole class passed into LMSR ownership. Nearly all, in fact, survived to have 40000 added to their numbers by BR. No 17454, built at St Rollox in 1897, was not to be scrapped until March 1953.

18 June 1936: Time stands still as ex-HR 'River' Class 4–6–0 No 14756 drifts into Ballinluig Junction with its Perth-Blair Athol 'slow'. First of six such engines designed by F. G. Smith during his short term of office, this engine, known then as HR No 70 *River Ness*, was one of only two actually delivered to the Highland Railway, for the latter's Civil Engineer, ostensibly concerned over his track and bridges, promptly banned the class on axle loading grounds. The poor HR sold them almost immediately to the Caledonian, whence they acquired both the nickname 'Hielmen' and running numbers 938–943. The ultimate irony came after Grouping. HR bridges and track were strengthened, and soon, restyled LMSR Nos 14756–761, Smith's massive 4–6–0s could be found working quite happily on former Highland territory. No doubt the older porter seen standing on Ballinluig's platform knew the whole sad story from A to Z . . .

18 June 1936 (2)

Ballinluig Junction, another victim of the Beeching axe, was closed eventually on 3 May 1965. No 14756 perished long before that, in November 1939.

18 June 1936 (3)

18 June 1936: Long before tourism became an industry the CR built a modest 5¼-mile branch between Killin Junction, on its Oban main line, and Loch Tay. The only intermediate station on the single-line branch was Killin

(4¼ miles), and a 20 mph speed limit applied along its length as it gradually descended to the shores of Loch Tay. The sole passing loop was at Loch Tay station; and, here, in the sylvan surroundings of the latter, ex-CR 0–4–4T No 15233, having brought in its two-coach train from Killin Junction, moves forward to enable its fireman to replenish his coal bunker. A second wagon of coal and a water column lie further behind, and Loch Tay's one-engine shed can also be seen. Passenger and freight services between Killin and Loch Tay were terminated by the LMSR on 11 September 1939, but similar services between Killin and Killin Junction were kept going until 28 September 1965. During that period, when BR Class '4' 2–6–4Ts finally took over, the track between Killin and Loch Tay stations was ash-filled between the rails to provide a convenient pathway for both local people and visitors. The only possible element of danger was a night-time one, when the branch engine, as of yore, sought refuge in Loch Tay's engine shed.

That same evening Le Manquais returned to Dundee. The next day found him at Arrochar and Tarbet, calmly photographing shipping! Twenty-four hours later one last photograph of 'Royal Scot' No 6111 *Royal Fusilier* heading a southbound express at Carlisle (Citadel) tells us at least how he got home after his momentous fortnight in Scotland. He must have found a vastly different scene when next he returned—in 1957.

CHAPTER SEVEN

THE IRISH SCENE

One is tempted to deduce from the number of times Le Manquais visited Ireland (seven in all over the years 1934–38) that he had family, or ancestral, connections there. But such, I am informed, was not the case. The man just loved Irish scenery— and Irish railways, North and South alike. Yet, carefully compiled though his note-books were, they do not always reveal just how he travelled there from the UK. More than once one finds him at (say) Great Missenden one day, and Dublin the next!

Fortunately, hints of a view or two taken from the deck of SS *Great Western* as that good vessel edged her overnight way into Waterford Harbour one June morn-ing in 1934 are all we need to tell us how Le Manquais *first* contrived to set foot on Irish soil. Equally clear indication that he was already *au fait* with Irish railway history is borne out by his swift descent on Waterford Manor Station, the home, since 1853, of one of southern Ireland's most intriguing 5ft 3in gauge minor railways. Operated by then, of course, by Great Southern Railways, he found that the one-time Waterford & Tramore Railway still retained many of its ancient characteristics, in-cluding that of being completely isolated from any other Irish railway.

9 June 1934: Although Waterford & Tramore Railway was absorbed by the GSR on 1 January 1925, the little railway's tradition of never running bunker-first was not abandoned. Hence, 2–2–2WT No 483, formerly W&TR No 1, having brought its Tramore train into Waterford Manor, is moving forward to the turntable before running round its train. The latter, incidentally, con-sisted of an articulated pair of 1928-vintage Clayton steam rail cars. The GSR removed their power bogies, and set them to work on the W&TR sec-tion in 1933. The venerable single-wheeler, Fairbairn-built in 1855 (Works No 55), might well have completed its century, but for the melancholy fact

9 June 1934

that, after derailment at Farriglog Bridge in August 1935, it was cut up on the spot. Irish railway preservationists still regard that decision as a grave error of judgement.

The next morning found Le Manquais in Cork, intent on travelling all the way to Bantry. But, even as he walked to Albert Quay station an interesting street scene caught his eye.

10 June 1934

10 June 1934: Passers-by in the city of Cork seem quite unconcerned as an ex-Great Southern & Western Railway 0–6–0T, bent on transferring a few vans from Albert Quay to Glanmire Road station, concedes right of way to horsedrawn traffic. Ahead lies one of two electrically operated lift bridges which crossed the River Lee. This unusual ¾-mile stretch of railway line, created by Cork City Railways in 1912, provided a link between Cork Bandon & South Coast Railway metals and those of GS&WR at Glanmire Road. Hopes that through passenger traffic might develop came to nought. Goods traffic, however, to and from the City and Albert Quay carried on, subject always to limitation of twenty wagons and a speed limit of 5 mph, until all was terminated in 1976.

Well aware that Cork Bandon metals had, fifty years earlier, provided a convenient springboard for two more Irish minor railways, Le Manquais broke his return journey from Bantry in quite leisurely fashion. Changing direction at Drimoleague Junction, he first pressed on to Baltimore, Ireland's southernmost rail point. Then, up he came to Skibbereen, where, still sharing the hospitality of the standard gauge station, the 3ft gauge metals of what was once the Schull & Skibbereen Tramways & Light Railway meandered off on their own errant way towards Schull, a fishing village 15½ miles distant. Operated from 1925 by the GSR, as were all railways contained exclusively within the Irish Free State, the Schull & Skibbereen, even from the very day it was opened in 1886, must rank as one of the most forlorn exercises in Irish railway history.

13 June 1934 (1)

13 June 1934: Seen here with its customary mixed train at Hollyhill, two stations out from Skibbereen, outside framed 4–4–0T No 1S, Peckett built

in 1906, still bears the name *Gabriel* that it carried when it served as Schull & Skibbereen No 1. One hour and ten minutes later, after running alongside public highways, hiving off occasionally over quite steepish gradients, and threading its way over a twelve-arched viaduct at Ballydehob, the train will drop to sea level at Schull, and deposit its meagre complement of passengers and freight. Two trains a day generally sufficed to meet demands in this sparsely populated area, and only the Irish government's concern for the local populace justified continuation of service under the GSR's wing. Even then, problems proved to be intractable, and rail services between Schull and Skibbereen were abandoned on 27 January 1947. *Gabriel* had already been withdrawn in 1936.

Determined to explore this fascinating corner of Ireland to the full, Le Manquais resumed his return journey to Cork as far as Clonakilty Junction. Thence he dropped south again to Ballinscarthy Junction, to gain access to the nine miles of the Timoleague & Courtmacsherry Extension Light Railway. Opened in 1891, the latter was really a 5ft 3in gauge roadside tramway. Sole justification again lay in serving small fishing villages and resorts on Ireland's south coast, and curves along a difficult route were such that the T&CELR's original bogie stock was carefully confined to 30ft in length.

13 June 1934 (2)

13 June 1934: Once the T&CELR was absorbed by the GSR in January 1925, ex-G&SWR 0–6–0T No 90, one of few locomotives light enough for the purpose, assisted for many years in maintaining local service; and is seen here at Courtmacsherry station. Built at Inchinore in 1876 as a 0–6–4T, with a carriage portion over its trailing bogie, the engine was designed by

A. Macdonnell for light passenger work on the Castleisland branch. Rebuilt in 0–6–0T form in 1915, it was little used on GSR's Timoleague branch after 1955; for by then only occasional excursions and a daily goods train were using the line. Withdrawn in 1959, No 90 was, however, subsequently placed on permanent exhibition at Mallow station.

Back in Cork two days later, Le Manquais paused only long enough to investigate the Cork & Muskerry, another vintage narrow-gauge line, before catching a train to Waterford, *via* Mallow. The latter was not without interest.

15 June 1934

15 June 1934: GSR 'K1' 2–6–0 No 382 presents a profile very familiar to southern English eyes as it pauses at Mallow station; and not without good reason. After World War 1 Woolwich Arsenal made a bid to relieve unemployment by constructing parts for 100 SECR-type 2–6–0 tender engines. In the event 27 sets were purchased by Irish railways, and from these emerged 26 GSR Moguls. The first twenty, given 5ft 6in driving wheels, and to all intents replicas of SECR's 'N' class, were numbered GSR 372–391. A further six Class 'K1As', built in 1930 and numbered 393–398, differed only by having 6ft wheels; and were thus identified with SR's 'U' Class. For some reason known only to GSR, No 392 was never built. Withdrawal of both classes commenced in 1955, and by 1962 all had gone.

That week in Ireland must have given Le Manquais immense satisfaction; for within a month he was back in Dublin for a few days. This time the Great Northern Railway (Ireland) whetted his interest with its electrically operated 5ft 3in gauge Hill of Howth Tramway.

The following year that south-west corner of Ireland again drew him like a magnet. Tantalizingly, he first comes to the surface at Tralee, where, needless to say, Ireland's most idiosyncratic 3ft gauge railway immediately invited his inspection. Its terminus and that of the main line lay only a few hundred yards apart.

15 June 1935

15 June 1935: Ex-Tralee & Dingle Light Railway No 2T (Hunslet 478/ 1889), an example of that railway's predilection for o/c 2–6–0Ts, is ready to leave Tralee Station with its typically mixed train. For the first ten miles life will not be difficult as the train weaves its way, tramwaywise, along country roadsides. West of Castlegregory Junction, however, subsequent climbs and descents at 1 in 30 will tax No 2T and her crew to the utmost, ere a last five miles of easier running sees them into Dingle Station.

Civil War in 1921, national fuel shortage in 1947, and, finally, bus competition all served to exacerbate T&D's already turbulent history; and rail service between Tralee and Dingle gradually dwindled into a monthly double-headed cattle train. Great events for enthusiasts, the last of these was hauled by Nos 1T and 2T in June 1953. It was their swan song; for both locos were scrapped at Inchinore immediately after.

Back on the main line, Valentia Harbour, Ireland's most westerly railway station, was Le Manquais' next target. The first stage in this spectacular journey involved a change of train at Farranfore Junction.

18 June 1935: Wisely, the fireman of No 182, one of GS&WR's ever popular '101' Class 0–6–0s, now GSR Class 'J15', tops up his water supply before backing on to his Valentia Harbour branch train of six-wheeled coaches. This 39¼-mile standard gauge link from Farranfore, penetrating deep into the bleak-looking heart of Co Kerry, cost over £8,000 a mile to build, and was opened in January 1885. Initial passenger service amounted to three

18 June 1935

mixed trains daily each way, and a running time of 2¾ hours was required. By 1954, however, service was sadly reduced to one, with additional passenger accommodation offered on a much slower daily goods! Even the introduction of diesel traction failed to achieve vitally required economies, and the Valentia branch finally closed on 30 January 1960.

A week later, after exhaustive survey of that south-west area, Le Manquais revisited Bantry. On this occasion Drimoleague Junction offered him a vintage reminder of yet another standard gauge minor railway.

25 June 1935

25 June 1935: By the late 1880s the city of Cork found itself served by five different railways, two of them 3ft in gauge. All maintained separate termini, and there was no physical connection between any two. Macroom, for instance, a country town of some 2,000 inhabitants, decided in 1861 to link itself to Cork by 5ft 3in gauge metals. Thus, the Cork & Macroom Direct Railway opened for public service on 12 May 1866. At first the new railway shared Cork Bandon station facilities at Albert Quay. Then, inevitably, disagreements arose, and Macroom opened its own terminus at Capwell, some distance away, in September 1879.

The C&MDR duly became part of the GSR in 1925 and, ten years later, this oil-lit four-wheeled Macroom coach, now numbered GSR 25R, could still be found at Drimoleague Junction. Despite GSR's commendable concern for country branches, a last train on the Macroom line ran on 10 November 1953.

Thence, content to spend the remaining four days of his holiday in familiar circumstances, Le Manquais returned to both Schull and Courtmacsherry territories. The latter provided him with a classic cameo of roadside tramway life in southern Ireland.

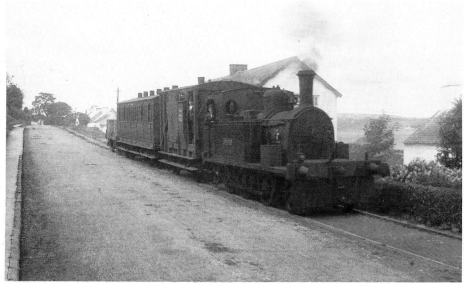

27 June 1935

27 June 1935: Many minor Irish railways had an endearing habit of pausing to pick up, or deposit, passengers by the roadside. Thus, the crew of *Argadeen*, T&CELR's unusual i/c 2-6-0T, were quite happy to linger long enough outside Courtmacsherry to afford Le Manquais his photograph. Judging by the makeup of the train, he may well have been the only passenger! The little engine, meanwhile, an 1894 product of Hunslet Engine Co of Leeds (Works No 611), was one of only three engines, all tanks, employed by T&CELR during its 34 years of independent existence. Somewhat unusually, GSR allowed two survivors to retain their names. So, numberless

to the end, *Argadeen* soldiered on until 1957, ten years after regular passenger services ceased between Timoleague and Courtmacsherry.

Later that year Le Manquais, exploring former Dublin & South Eastern Railway metals, spent a week at Bray. Came 1936, however, and holidays in Holland and Scotland confined his Irish attentions to a very brief reacquaintance with Howth, the GNR(I) junction just north of Dublin. Still, within a period of two years he had succeeded in travelling on four major constituent companies of the GSR—G&SWR, MGWR, D&ESR, and Cork Bandon—two minor 5ft 3in GSR absorptions, W&TR and T&CELR, and four of the six 3ft gauge Irish Free State railways. That said, it was hardly surprising that he decided, in 1937, to devote a fortnight to the northern half of what was once the Kingdom of Ireland.

The exercise proved to be a formidable, and much more complicated, proposition. Starting at Portrush, almost as far north as he could get, he briefly sampled the Giant's Causeway Tramway. Two days later he was at Tynan, birthplace of the Clogher Valley Railway, a second Northern Irish 'lost cause', in that both GCT and CVR were allowed by Stormont to fade into oblivion in the 1940s. Poor CVR, it had hardly experienced a troublefree year since its inception as a 3ft gauge tramway in 1887.

15 June 1937 (1)

15 June 1937: For a 3ft gauge railway which crammed 37 stations and halts into its 37-mile length, the Clogher Valley Railway was remarkably generous in its construction of major stations. This view of Clogher station makes the point. The engine, CVR No 4, bound for Tynan, is equally interesting, being a 2–6–2 reconstruction of a 2–6–0T (Hudswell Clarke No 698/1904) which,

formerly employed by Castlederg & Victoria Bridge Tramway, became the subject of a barter deal between CVR and scrap merchants in 1934. In addition to fitting a trailing bogie, Clogher workshops removed the loco's one-sided metal skirting, and added a new bunker in lieu of boiler-top coal hoppers. The latter luxury enabled No 4 to work boiler-first—a distinct relief from traditional CVR tramway practice of running cab-first—and the reborn tank remained a popular asset right to the bitter end in 1942, when CVR was forced to close.

15 June 1937 (2)

15 June 1937: Also seen at Clogher was CVR's diesel rail car No 1. Supplied by Walker Bros in 1932, it and a diesel tractor purchased the following year were the fruits of Henry Forbes' enthusiasm as one of two government representatives on a committee of management which had been appointed in 1928 to monitor CVR's ailing affairs. The coach body, articulated from the power unit, could seat 28 passengers, and the 74 hp six-cylinder Gardner diesel engine was powerful enough to take on an additional coach as required. During their first twelve months the diesels took care of 35,000 miles, and, with steam adding a further 34,000, it was, no doubt, the cost savings of the former which enabled CVR to totter on for a few more years. When the end did come Forbes was shrewd enough to acquire both diesels for further service on his own Co Donegal Railway.

Considering that travel along the full length of the CVR demanded a premium of three hours or more, one can understand Le Manquais' relief at being able to switch to the comparative luxury of a GNR(I) coach at Macguiresbridge. Soon, however, he was out again; at Enniskillen, where the near juxtaposition of Sligo Leitrim & Northern Counties Rly veteran 0–6–4T *Leitrim* and GNR(I)'s petrol-engine railbus 'D' simply could not be ignored. Eventually, he changed at Bundoran Junction, and pushed further west.

16 June 1937 (1)

16 June 1937: Pettigo Station lay almost on the shores of Lough Erne, and was situated halfway along a 35½-mile branch which separated Bundoran Junction and the Donegal Bay watering places of Bundoran and Ballyshannon. The single-line branch was opened by Enniskillen & Bundoran Railway on 13 June 1866, but was worked by Irish & North Western Railway. Latterly both railways passed into GNR(I) ownership; which explains why GNR(I) 'U' Class 4–4–0 No 199 is now seen entering Pettigo's passing loop on semi-express duty. As Bundoran lay in Co Donegal, and was, therefore, part of the Irish Free State, delay at *two* Customs stations lay ahead for 199 and its train. No 199 was later named *Lough Derg*, and the line itself was closed on 30 September 1957.

We shall never know the true extent of the agonies which befell Irish railways after the 1921 Partition and the 'Troubles' which followed. The Free State, being one-nation minded, grouped most of its railways, standard and narrow-gauge alike, under GSR aegis: Ulster, more sympathetic towards private ownership, and less impressed by the role railways could play in scattered communities, allowed individual companies to continue their own way. Meanwhile, for quite different, and rather tragic, reasons, Ireland's two largest narrow-gauge concerns, Co Donegal Railways Joint Committee and the Londonderry & Lough Swilly Railway, were disowned by both governments—simply because eighteen miles of track belonging to the former, and 2¼ miles of the latter, lay in Northern Ireland. Neither, therefore, could be incorporated wholly within GSR jurisdiction.

Le Manquais' first contact with the CDJRC came at Ballyshannon, where evidence of the supreme fight Henry Forbes, the committee's secretary, was putting up

for rail survival soon came to light. Like our own Colonel Stephens, Forbes believed
that the fortunes of country railways could be revived by introducing railcar flexi-
bility. Unlike poor Stephens, however, Forbes had the backing of company re-
sources. After initial experiments with petrol-engine railcars, Forbes triumphantly
introduced, in 1931, the first diesel engine railcars in the British Isles.

16 June 1937 (2)

16 June 1937: CDRJC railcars Nos 7 and 8, built in 1931, were powered by
Gardner 74 hp diesel engines. True to Henry Forbes' ambitions, they ran
16/17 miles to the gallon, and produced gross operating costs of 3½d per
mile, as opposed to steam's 10½d. They were also robust enough to haul a
light van or two, as can be seen from this Ballyshannon photograph of No 7.
Built at a cost of £2,086 each, the two railcars' undoubted success paved the
way for the introduction of five more diesel cars by the time No 7 was withdrawn in 1949. Interestingly, CDRJC's last two diesel railcars, purchased in
1950–51, now function happily in the Isle of Man.

Finding his way to Strabane eventually, Le Manquais then enjoyed a more conventional Co Donegal scene.

17 June 1937: Co Donegal Railway, with a route mileage of 105½, owned
Ireland's most extensive 3ft gauge system by 1905. Purchased jointly by
Midland Railway and GNR(I) the following year, it was thereafter run by
CDRJC. Nevertheless, Co Donegal's penchant for tank locomotives was
maintained when CDRJC ordered five 2–6–4Ts from Nasmyth Wilson in
1907. One of them, No 17 *Glenties* (No 829/1907) is seen here at Strabane
station with a typical two-coach train. With outside bearings and
Walschaerts valve gear, these highly successful locomotives marked a radical
departure from previous Co Donegal practice.

17 June 1937

This, too, may well have been a last chance to photograph *Glenties*; for later that year, when CDRJC stock was renumbered and some old Donegal Railway names were revived, the engine re-emerged as No 5 *Drumboe*. When CDRJC operations finally ceased on 31 December 1959 *Drumboe* was one of several tanks purchased by an American, Dr Ralph Cox. Unfortunately, the purchaser could not implement his good intentions, and, dumped in Strabane station yard in 1961, *Drumboe* has lain there rusting ever since.

Lacking a Henry Forbes at its head, the Londonderry & Lough Swilly, Ireland's second largest narrow-gauge railway at 96¾ route miles, stayed exclusively with steam in its post-Second World War battle against bus competition. Its main line offered a desolate haul of 74½ miles from Londonderry to Burtonport, on the Atlantic coast, and it says much for Le Manquais' stamina that we find him at Burtonport forty-eight hours after visiting Strabane. At Gweedore, on the return journey, he caught up with one of Lough Swilly's more remarkable engines.

19 June 1937: The railway world was duly impressed in 1905 when L&LSR commissioned Hudswell Clarke to supply two massive 3ft gauge 4–8–0 tender locomotives for use on mixed traffic work between Londonderry and Burtonport. No 11 was scrapped in 1933, but No 12 was still serving when this photograph was taken at Gweedore station.

Engine and tender weighed 58¼ tons, but, seen at platform level, their narrow-gauge proportions are self evident. Once the two potential passengers, and the boxes of Liverpool-bound fish, have been taken on board, No 12 and its mixed train will set off on the laborious 3½-hour journey, eastward and across the Irish Free State border, to Londonderry. It was, of course, this unforgivable dual role which eventually crucified the Lough Swilly in 1953.

19 June 1937

Indefatigable as ever, Le Manquais then moved back east, calmly photographed Fintona's famous horse-drawn tramway, and, entering NCC territory, worked his way to Ballycastle, in the far north—all within a space of four days.

24 June 1937

24 June 1937: A relic of former days, when Belfast & Northern Counties Railway ruled its own roost, and its young locomotive engineer, Bowman Malcolm, introduced two handsome narrow-gauge Beyer Peacock com-

pound 2–4–2Ts (1892). B&NCR was itself taken over by NCC eleven years later, and a similar tank, seen here at Ballycastle, was built at York Road, Belfast shops in 1908. Three more followed between 1909 and 1920. The one in our photograph saw many changes. Originally numbered 112, it was renumbered 102 in 1920, and, yet again, 42 in 1939. Meanwhile, initially classified 'S' by NCC, a bunker added behind its cab in 1928 saw it reclassified 'S1'.

Half an hour after this picture was taken No 102 backed on to its train of two bogie coaches and half a dozen wagons and vans, and left to link up with NCC's main line at Ballymoney, 16¼ miles away. By 1949, though, NCC's overlordship vanished in favour of Ulster Transport Authority, and all operations on this increasingly unprofitable narrow gauge section ceased in 1950.

In his last trip to Ireland, in 1938, Le Manquais again entered *via* Waterford; and this time he sampled the trip to Tramore, behind ex-MGWR 0–6–0T No 555, which had, by now, taken the single wheeler's place. Because of Waterford & Tramore's unique isolation, this and two similar tanks had to be delivered to a siding at Waterford South station, whence they were steamed to Waterford Manor along sections of rail laid along 1¾ miles of public highway! At least they lasted in service until 1955.

Having exhausted the joys of Waterford, on went Le Manquais, through Limerick Junction, to Limerick itself—then Ennis, deep in Co Clare. Here, GSR platform facilities were shared by yet another Irish narrow-gauge railway, the West Clare.

5 July 1938

5 July 1938: Some Irish 3ft gauge railways led an independent existence; others earned a living by 'feeding' off Ireland's main lines. The West &

South Clare Railways, both incorporated in 1884, elected to belong to the latter category by deliberately choosing Ennis, the county town of Clare, as their springboard. Here, at Ennis station, GSR Class 'D17' 4–4–0 No 57 has arrived on a Limerick-Athenry train. A few passengers have alighted, and West Clare 2–6–2T No 2C, formerly *Ennis* (T. Green & Son, Leeds No 234/1900), waits hopefully in the narrow-gauge bay (right) for any last minute bonus before embarking on its three-hour, 48 mile-long trip to Kilkee. Dieselization ultimately brought the journey time down to 2 hr 20 min: but it was all too late, and the last 3ft gauge railway to function in Ireland, the West & South Clare, closed down completely in 1961.

From there Le Manquais went on to enjoy both railways and scenery in the locality. He finished up where he started in 1934—at Waterford. Thus, other interesting railway pictures followed. But, somehow, here, pushed for space, that combined standard and narrow-gauge memory of Ennis seems as appropriate a way as any to conclude our brief glimpse of Irish railway life in the 1930s.

CHAPTER EIGHT

COLONEL STEPHENS' RAILWAYS

On 23 October 1931, in somewhat distressing circumstances, there passed from our midst one of the most engaging figures in the history of British railway administration. One uses the word 'administration' advisedly—for Holman Frederick Stephens was no dashing locomotive engineer. Nevertheless, a passion for local rail transport, plus an earlier education in civil engineering and a military-like flair for discipline and organization, combined within him to help create a unique light railway 'empire'. Typical of the man, it was all ruled with military precision, varying degrees of success, and bouts of (largely Welsh-inspired) exasperation, from a modest office in Quarry Road, Tonbridge, Kent.

The fact that Stephens' 'empire' was, despite its late infusion of Welsh blood, essentially English in character must, I fear, suffice to explain why, throughout the Colonel's career, I, and many more up in Scotland, remained blissfully unaware that the man ever existed. More fool us! Fortunately, there *were* enthusiasts further south who took considerable pains to record the passing light railway scene. Le Manquais, as it happened, was one of the later 'pioneers'; and I find it rather touching that in the year 1933, poised as he was on the brink of an exciting career in electronics, he could still find time, and energy, to pursue a keen investigative interest in the light railway legacy the gallant Colonel left behind. By then the empire was safely in the keeping of Stephens' trusted lieutenant, W. H. Austen.

Le Manquais' involvement started with a visit to Chichester, where, so beguiled must he have been by the prospect of viewing the West Sussex Light Railway in action, that he quite forgot to photograph the ex-LB&SCR station which lay alongside the minor railway's much humbler establishment. That, in itself, is interesting—for he rarely missed a trick! The WSLR at that time, though deteriorating fast, was still

running a few trains daily. Ergo, Le Manquais lost no time in hastening next door to see what delights the one-time Hundred of Manhood & Selsey Tramway had to offer.

Stephens' connection with the standard-gauge tramway began just before World War 1, when he was appointed Engineer. Built without Parliamentary hindrance on private land, and opened to traffic on 27 August 1897, the tramway was subsequently 'rationalized' under a Light Railway Order in 1924, when, too—and here, surely, we can detect the Stephens 'touch'—it acquired a new title, the West Sussex Light Railway. So potent, indeed, did the Stephens factor become, that the Colonel, when he died, was Chairman, Managing Director, Engineer, and Locomotive Superintendent, all in one. No doubt Le Manquais spotted many a constructional hallmark when he first set eyes on WSLR's Chichester station.

26 September 1933 (1)

26 September 1933: The former Selsey Tramway, its 7½-mile length packed with nine intermediate stations—two of them private halts which were not even mentioned in Company timetables—maintained an equally cheerful eccentricity where termini were concerned. Chichester and Selsey Town may have shared the distinction of being the only gas-lit stations on the line: but Selsey, serving much the smaller town, was always regarded as the more important terminus. Station and yard occupied an area of 2½ acres, and here locomotives and rolling stock were serviced.

It follows that as the tramway's aging stock of secondhand tank engines began to display an ever-increasing tendency to falter in the course of duty, the inspection pit seen in this general view of Chichester station assumed growing importance in day-to-day operations. Engine No 5 *Ringing Rock*, a Manning Wardle 0–6–0ST built in 1883, has, for instance, just vacated the pit, and is filling up with water at the far end of the station before venturing to resume duties with its one-coach Selsey train. The light spiked track, sadly

in need of attention, and the corrugated iron station building were also very characteristic of the kind of 'lame duck' enterprise Colonel Stephens strove so valiantly to revive.

The very piquancy of the Chichester scene probably strengthened Le Manquais' resolve to embark on a journey to Selsey for himself. Once *Ringing Rock* recovered composure sufficiently to re-present herself and solitary coach at the platform, off he went. Judging by a shaky photograph or two he snatched *en route*, he enjoyed what might truthfully be described as a 'rattling good trip'!

Hunston, Sidlesham, classic names both in Selsey Tram history, slid by, and eventually Le Manquais found himself at Selsey. There, he found, the impact of a much more spacious environment was soon offset by an air of positive dereliction which hung about the place. Over in the station yard passenger and freight stock lay rotting in the sun, and with no one about to stay his progress—a useful prerequisite, incidentally, if ever one chose to trespass on Colonel Stephens territory—he strolled across to investigate:

26 September 1933 (2)

26 September 1933: This handsome coach, now mouldering away at Selsey, was one of three four-wheeled ex-Lambourn Valley Railway vehicles purchased by the tramway from the GWR in 1910. 26½ft long, and finished in varnished wood, it seated 32 first and second class passengers. The latter, though, had to be content with wooden seating. A central gangway leading to platforms at each end enabled the guard to pass along the length of the train, and steps assisted passengers to board or alight at low-platformed halts. The carriage behind in this view was one of a pair of ex-LCDR six-wheelers bought later. The hulk on the right was typical of a score or so WSLR goods vehicles which had also been dumped in Selsey Town yard.

26 September 1933: When Selsey Tramway opened for public use in 1897

26 September 1933 (3)

its passenger stock consisted solely of three Falcon-built cars. 37ft long, and running on two outside-framed four-wheeled bogies, each had a saloon compartment, seating 48 passengers, and a separate luggage compartment. A central corridor necessitated transverse seating, and doors at both ends opened on to covered platforms. Originally liveried in crimson lake, the three pioneer vehicles were later supplemented by the arrival of a similar carriage, built by Hurst Nelson. Here, decades later, the Hurst Nelson coach itself lies derelict in Selsey Town yard. Rather poignantly, despite the ravages of wind and sun, the name 'Selsey Tramway' still just shows on the board beneath the central windows.

Whatever Le Manquais' emotions were that day, he could hardly have cavilled at the WSLR's parting gesture, for he travelled all the way back to Chichester in one of Colonel Stephens' immortal 'innovations'—the little railway's Shefflex rail-car. Introduced only five years previously, it had replaced an even more eccentric prototype, a Wolseley-Siddeley petrol-driven rail bus. Needless to say, there was little to choose between the noise and vibration each created as it ground its way along light railway metals. Meanwhile, safe if not unshaken, Le Manquais had the presence of mind to employ his camera the moment he arrived at Chichester:

26 September 1933: WSLR's rail-car unit, seen here at Chichester, consisted of two Shefflex vehicles, operated back to back, though often separated by an open utility wagon. Bodies were built by W. J. Flear of Sheffield and the cars were assembled by Shefflex Motor Co of Tinsley. Each had seating for 23 passengers. Power, meantime, was provided by two four-cylinder engines, and petrol was gravity-fed from underseat fourteen-gallon tanks. The driver sat in conventional bus fashion, and speeds depended on his skill in manipulating three forward gears. Luggage went on top, and seat-

26 September 1933 (4)

ing was designed to allow provision of a gangway down the centre of each car. Designwise, twin headlights and a central buffer added an almost-sophisticated element, particularly when compared to the Colonel's earlier innovations, and, despite the presence of a bell in front of the dashboard, additional warning to lineside transgressors was given by a whistle attached to the exhaust. In practice, the noise of a rail-car's approach was quite sufficient to alert the whole neighbourhood!

Le Manquais' next contact with a Colonel Stephens railway consisted of a very brief flirtation with the Kent & East Sussex Railway early in 1935. He must have been intent on reaching some other destination when he passed through Rolvenden, for he only paused long enough to capture one locomotive before pressing on. Yet, by a strange coincidence that photograph includes an engine that had once borne a name that he had encountered on another locomotive two years earlier.

14 April 1935: K&ESR engine No 8, seen here in splendid isolation at Rolvenden, also bore the name *Ringing Rock* when Manning Wardle supplied it to the Narberth Road & Maenclochog Railway in 1876. After a decade during which the little Welsh railway was closed, the saddle tank re-entered service under North Pembrokeshire & Fishguard Railway auspices in 1895; and, three years later, the GWR assumed control. Rebuilt, as GWR No 1380, at Swindon in 1902, then withdrawn and sold to the Bute Supply Co in 1912, the engine ultimately became No 8 on the K&ESR. Stephens, with his classical education, favoured classical names—so the new acquisition was christened *Hesperus*. The name had been removed by the time the above study was taken; but No 8's self-evident GWR lines remained with it until withdrawal came in 1941.

14 April 1935

In the autumn of the following year Le Manquais made acquaintance with a Stephens' 'classic'—the Colonel's first venture into narrow-gauge railway construction. On this occasion he remembered to photograph SR's ex-SECR station before stepping out: and thence, no doubt, he had little difficulty in spotting the well-advertised roof of Rye & Camber Tramway's station as it huddled at sea level, well below the town ramparts.

Stephens was only 27 when he was appointed Engineer to this odd little railway. It opened on 13 July 1895 employing conventional steam haulage, despite Stephens' intention of utilizing an internal combustion locomotive along its mere 1½ mile 3ft gauge length. A Bagnall-built 2–4–0T, bearing the appropriate name *Camber*, and one semi-open carriage performed the honours, and early success persuaded the R&CT directors to obtain another 2–4–0T and carriage in 1897. Built entirely on private land, and intended primarily as a means of transport for golfers and the Rye Harbour community, the tramway, with its 261b Vignoles rails spiked to creosoted wooden sleepers, and corrugated-iron generously employed on station buildings at either end, epitomized much of Stephens' future light railway practice. For him economy spelt survival.

In July 1908 one more mile was added to the tramway, the original Camber terminus was renamed Golf Links, and a new, somewhat spartan, station was opened at Camber Sands. Then in 1925, influenced probably by Stephens, whose advisory services had been retained, the Tramway acquired a four-wheeled petrol locomotive. *Victoria*, the younger of the Tramway's two steam locomotives was promptly sold for scrap. As the 1930s progressed, however, the increasing use of private cars, and the institution of a bus service betwen Rye and Camber, saw *Camber*, the surviving steam locomotive, banished almost permanently to Rye shed. Thus, by the time Le Manquais arrived on the scene, the 'Lawnmower', as the petrol loco was known locally, was in sole charge of a sadly reduced service:

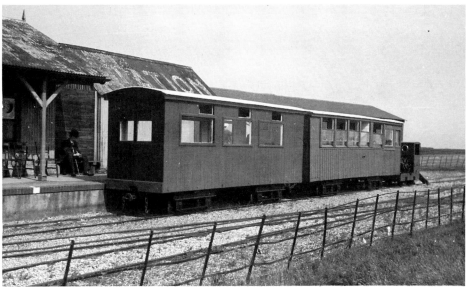

16 August 1936 (1)

16 August 1936: Rye & Camber's little petrol locomotive, supplied by Kent Construction Co of Ashford in 1925, prepares to leave Rye station with the tramway's total passenger stock, two wooden-bodied bogie coaches. That farthest from the camera, 25½ft long and Bagnall-built for the opening of the line in 1895, had platforms, now boarded in, at each end. Reduced in modern times to exclusive third class use, it once seated twelve first class and twenty second class passengers. The other coach, built locally in 1896, had fewer windows, and its 24ft length, with access at one end only, always accommodated 25 third class passengers. Each vehicle was fitted with a handbrake, and weighed 3 tons empty. Entrance on one side only met R&C requirements, and glass panes in the sash windows were removable as summer conditions permitted.

In this view the sole occupant of Rye station 'waiting room', an elderly gentleman, appears to be either resting, or contemplating the journey which lies ahead . . .

Evidently, Le Manquais joined him, for his next photograph takes us farther down the line:

16 August 1936: End of the line, though only 2½ miles from Rye, Camber Sands station opened on 13 July 1908 with a bare wooden-sleepered platform. The small waiting room was later installed as a much needed protection against wind and sand. Meanwhile, in forlorn anticipation of extra summer traffic, a brace of wagons, fitted with cross-benches, have been added to the normal stock complement. The conductor is chatting with the only passenger in sight, while the driver, immaculate as ever in yachting cap, hopefully scans the horizon. The station run-round loop was a common feature throughout the R&CT, which, of course, was completely devoid of signals.

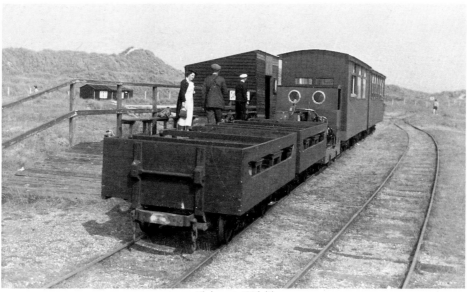

16 August 1936 (2)

Already on its last legs, the tramway eventually closed just before war erupted in 1939. Damage done to its metals during military occupation ensured that it never re-opened.

* * *

Came Spring 1937, and Le Manquais could not resist revisiting the Kent & East Sussex Railway. Faced with a choice of joining it at either southern or northern end, he opted for the latter. His reward when he reached Headcorn—or Headcorn Junction, as the K&ESR insisted on calling it—was another trip behind a Shefflex set. Patently, he was back on Colonel Stephens territory!

In truth, he was back on the Colonel's favourite railway, for Rother Valley Railway's initial ten miles of standard gauge metals, opened between Robertsbridge and Tenterden on 26 March 1900, constituted Stephens' first constructional venture under the Light Railways Act of 1896. But once the line was extended one more mile, in 1903, to reach the present-day Tenterden station, and a majestic change of name to Kent & East Sussex Railway was effected the following year, the ambitions of Stephens, by now managing director, and his board began to run riot—and certainly far ahead of whatever funds were at their disposal. Further extensions to Cranbrook, Appledore, Pevensey and Rye were duly considered, but never built. A large Hawthorn tank, specially ordered to handle a proposed extension to Maidstone, duly arrived in 1904. Construction of such a heavily graded line, of course, proved quite beyond K&ESR's means, and *Hecate*, as a consequence, lingered as a pure 'white elephant' at Rolvenden for almost three decades. Stephens resisted any attempts at sale, and the impasse was only resolved in 1932, when W. H. Austen, as Official Receiver to the K&ESR, repaid a debt owed to Southern Railway by exchanging *Hecate* for some older stock.

Meanwhile, in the midst of all this drama, a final 10-mile extension from

Tenterden to Headcorn, on the Tonbridge–Ashford line of SECR, *was* opened on 15 May 1905. Unlike earlier Rother Valley track, this section was built to SER standards, and it was these more substantial metals which now beckoned Le Manquais as he photographed the Shefflex at Headcorn:

27 March 1937 (1)

27 March 1937: Reluctant to depart from Headcorn Junction totally devoid of passengers, the driver/conductor of K&ESR's Shefflex set tries hard to woo a potential customer, who, as yet, is keeping a safe distance while he ponders the problem. The Shefflex, similar in pedigree to that seen at Chichester, was introduced in 1930 following a successful earlier experiment by Colonel Stephens with two converted Ford road buses, linked, likewise, back to back. In its original form the Shefflex boasted twin headlights and a strongly mounted central buffer; but both refinements have vanished now in favour of a single roof headlight, and what looks like a klaxon horn. In typical light railway fashion, an open wagon trails at the rear.

27 March 1937: In this view of Rolvenden station, taken looking towards Headcorn, two of the three items received in exchange for *Hecate* can be spotted: the composite ex-LSWR bogie brake which is standing at the platform, and, on shed, ex-LSWR Beyer Peacock 0-6-0ST, formerly SR No E0335, now K&ESR No 4. In Rother Valley days this station bore the name Tenterden; then, in 1903, the latter village acquired a larger brick-built station of its own. Line operations were thereafter conducted from the general office there, though engine shed and repair shops remained centralized at the newly renamed Rolvenden. By the mid-1930s, as K&ESR resorted more and more to hiring SR locos, Rolvenden yard became a classic 'dump' for aban-

27 March 1937 (2)

doned K&ESR stock. During this visit, for instance, Le Manquais found a heavy ex-Midland Railway loco dept crane rusting away behind the loco shed. So, too, were the remains of K&ESR's Pickering steam rail car, once a source of great pride to Colonel Stephens. Ironically, the debris was not cleared, and track repaired, until war broke out in 1939.

From there Le Manquais appears to have walked to Tenterden, where he resumed his quiet investigation:

27 March 1937 (3)

27 March 1937: In sharp contrast to the state of affairs at Rolvenden, Tenterden station yard was innocent of 'junk'. Certainly, another Colonel Stephens acquisition, this handsome ex-North London Railway four-wheeled brake, now No 15 in K&ESR carriage stock, looked in good enough condition to be in current use. It lasted, in fact, until the British Transport Commission took over in 1948.

27 March 1937 (4)

27 March 1937: Tenterden station's more substantial construction and its newly-painted white canopy show to advantage in this study, as K&ESR No 3, rather optimistically equipped with express headlamps, waits to take its one-coach train on to Robertsbridge. Only 'Terriers' were allowed to work this lightly-laid section of the line. Symptomatic of H. F. Stephens' lifelong affection for the breed, No 3, then No 70 *Poplar*, was bought from LB&SCR for £650 in 1901, and was renamed *Bodiam* by Rother Valley Railway. A second 'Terrier', purchased similarly in 1905, entered K&ESR service as No 5 *Rolvenden*, but, unlike No 3, did not live to enter BR Southern Region locomotive stock.

After such a splendid day Le Manquais could not resist taking that train to Robertsbridge, and he finished his film with a 'shot' which captures much of the plangent nature of Colonel Stephens' light railway ambitions. It might well have been taken in Edwardian days:

27 March 1937: At SR's Robertsbridge station the east side of an island platform was reserved for K&ESR arrivals. Engine No 3, with its ex-LSWR bogie brake, plus sundry goods vehicles picked up *en route*, duly obliges—and discharges a typically disappointing complement of passengers. Six years later

27 March 1937 (5)

SR came to the rescue of the now failing 'Terrier' by offering an AIX boiler. Two KESR fitters attended St Leonards to assist. Then in May 1947 No 3 was given a complete overhaul at Brighton Works, and entered BR stock, lively as ever, as No 32670 the following year. By all rights it should have finished its days on Hayling Island branch service in 1963. By an appropriate stroke of good fortune, however, the little loco was saved from the breakers yard by Kent & East Sussex Preservation Society. Nowadays, in a perfect tribute to Colonel Stephens' memory, it operates, again as K&ESR No 3 *Bodiam*, along familiar metals between Tenterden and Bodiam.

Stephens fought many a rearguard action in his day. But none, perhaps, were more gallant than the challenge he accepted in 1907 of revitalizing the long moribund Potteries, Shrewsbury & North Wales Railway, or the battle he subsequently fought in trying to spare its successor, the Shropshire & Montgomeryshire Light Railway, a similar fate. Examine the latter's history how you will, and all the Stephens qualities are seen to emerge.

Possibly, but for the general economic harshness of the 1930s, creation of the S&MLR might well have ranked as his crowning achievement. Within eighteen months of the appropriate Light Railway Order being issued, every inch of the old 'Potts' main line between Llanymynech and Shrewsbury was relaid under his leadership. Nine existing stations were completely refurbished, six new halts were built; and all was rendered spic and span for ceremonial opening on 13 April 1911. A year later the 6-mile branch between Kinnerley and Criggion quarries was restored—this time for public use as well. 'Support the local line', he urged. Two new 0-6-2Ts were even purchased from Hawthorn Leslie to help embellish line operations. Alas, both proved too heavy for the S&MLR's lightly laid track, and had to be sold in 1914.

No doubt stifling a pang of regret, Stephens contented himself thereafter with adding further to the *mélange* of secondhand items which already formed the bulk of SM&LR stock. Thus, running true to form, three railcars, fifteen steam locomotives, nineteen secondhand coaches, and fifty assorted wagons, also of various parentage, ultimately found employment on S&MLR metals. Prominent amongst his locomotive 'bargains', three ex-LSWR 'Ilfracombe Goods' 0–6–0s, three ex-LB&SCR 'Terrier' tanks, and three ex-LNWR Webb coal engines all played their part in the S&MLR's fluctuating fortunes.

It worked, of course—while Stephens lived. But the twin misfortunes of Stephens' death and the wretched conditions which befell small railways in the 1930s confronted his successor, W. H. Austen, with such overwhelming odds that an almost immediate run-down of the S&MLR could not be averted. By the early 1930s one engine in steam met total daily requirements. Then passenger traffic was terminated in November 1933; and, by the end of 1937, only five steam engines remained. They, and such items of S&MLR coaching stock as survived, soon lay rusting in Kinnerley yard.

In light of the above one cannot help a feeling of regret that Le Manquais found himself unable to visit the Shropshire & Montgomeryshire scene until 16 April 1938. Still, considering that he spent the whole of the previous day prowling around the Manchester Ship Canal, the dear chap can hardly be faulted on grounds of either industry or mobility . . .

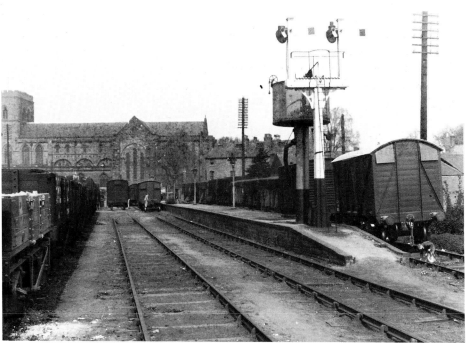

16 April 1938 (1)

16 April 1938: The presence at Shrewsbury Abbey Foregate station of a boy 'scrumping' coal, and a second visitor (centre background) examining a platelayer's trolley, underlines the demise of passenger traffic on the

Shropshire & Montgomeryshire Light Railway. Now only occasional coal and freight trains to intermediate stations, one weekly stone train, and very infrequent enthusiast-chartered 'specials' disturbed the peace of what was once the grandest station on the line when the 'Potts' railway opened in 1896. Yet, ironically, the years from 1941 onwards were to witness a remarkable transformation of traffic, once the Army installed dumps and sidings all along the main line. Slump, however, returned with derequisition in 1959, and on 29 February 1960 the line was officially closed. Abbey station site later became a permanent way and oil tank depot. Fortunately, the water tower seen in our picture was salvaged by Tenterden Railway Co.

Again, Le Manquais must have followed the line on foot; for his camera was next employed at Shrewsbury West, one mile out from Abbey station. It was one of the new halts created by Stephens in 1911 and its modest platform still carried quite a number of enamelled advertisements—mute reminders of Colonel Stephens' vigorous marketing policies. A little further on came other evidence of Stephens' economy and enterprise.

16 April 1938 (2)

16 April 1938: In its original form the 'Potts' main line was laid with double track. Sober reassessment, however, of traffic potential soon saw it singled. In this view, taken a little further west of Shrewsbury, the original track bed can still be seen. So, too, can twin bridges which crossed the GWR/LNWR line to Hereford (nearest the camera) and the GWR's line to Bridgnorth. Note how Stephens, in reconstructing the old line, used girders from the unemployed side to strengthen the other half of both bridges.

16 April 1938: During official consideration of the proposed S&MLR main line a second Light Railway Order, dated July 1910, authorized junction with

16 April 1938 (3)

the existing GWR/LNWR Wellington line at Meole Brace, 1¾ miles from Shrewsbury. Quick to take the LRO at its word, Stephens not only built a new station at Meole Brace, optimistically complete with booking office, but added exchange sidings. Here S&MLR trains of stone from Criggion quarries were handed over to GWR and LNWR care. In the event Meole Brace exchange sidings lasted longer than the S&MLR itself and were not closed until 1960.

After Meole Brace, unfortunately, Le Manquais, concerned to reach Welshpool that evening, denied himself the pleasure of a visit to Kinnerley and chose instead to cut straight across to Llanymynech.

16 April 1938 (4)

16 April 1938: At Llanymynech, eighteen miles from Shrewsbury, S&MLR's station adjoined that of the GWR, whose Welshpool-Oswestry trains utilized two platforms off-left in this picture. S&MLR's single line from Kinnerley swept in, meanwhile, and widened to accommodate Up and Down platforms. In earlier 'Potts' days a locomotive shed and turntable lay in the triangle behind the water tower. When this photograph was taken the junction with the GWR at the south end of the station (behind the camera) still existed—despite the fact that a lease over the once important 'Potts' Nantmawr mineral branch to which it gave access had been ceded to Cambrian Railways almost forty years earlier.

Colonel Stephens' advertising, though forthright, was never dishonest. One cannot help wondering, none the less, how many passengers, seduced by Stephens' proud platform boast, gaily embarked on the 'Shortest Route to Shrewsbury'—only to find themselves embroiled in a noisy boneshaking hour-long journey in a Ford railbus . . !

It was as well Le Manquais turned his attention to the Weston, Clevedon & Portishead Light Railway in April 1939; for that little railway closed down just over a year later. Only too typical of the Colonel Stephens saga, ailing receipts, plus a pressing creditor, applied the *coup de grâce*.

As far back as 1885 flotation of a tramway had been urged by local interests, who resented the fact that while Weston-super-Mare, Clevedon and Portishead each had access to the GWR's Bristol-Taunton main line there was no direct rail link between the three growing towns. Despite difficulty in raising capital, a tramway duly opened, on 1 December 1897, between Weston and Clevedon, a distance of 8½ miles; and passengers to Portishead were taken on by horse-drawn omnibus until a further 5½-mile extension was added ten years later. Meanwhile, two years after inauguration the tramway converted itself into a light railway by private Act, dated 9 August 1899.

The company paid dearly for that Portishead extension. Within a year it found itself in deep financial difficulty. In 1909 the Excess Insurance Company, who had been rash enough to take over major debts owed by the light railway, called in a receiver. The following year the GWR, when approached, declined to work, or purchase, the ailing concern. Next, compounding the gloom, WC&PR's General Manager, G. S. Newton, chose to emigrate to Canada in 1911. It was at this critical juncture that H. F. Stephens stepped in as his successor.

Poor Stephens! It was not one of his happiest ventures. Despite subsequent use of internal combustion vehicles in his fight against road competition, traffic on the WC&PR grew steadily sparser. Left unaffected by Grouping in 1923, the light railway struggled on; and it was really something of a miracle that the WC&PR was still functioning when Le Manquais paid a visit to the locality in 1939. He chose to plunge in at the Weston end:

8 April 1939: One of the very few fixed signals to be found on the WC&PR confronts Drewry car No 2 as it waits to leave Weston station. On this occasion it was hauling the modest unpowered trailer more normally associated with smaller Drewry petrol rail car No 1. The latter was purchased

8 April 1939 (1)

new by WC&PR in 1922, and, evidence of Colonel Stephens' continued enthusiasm for petrol-engined rail transport, Drewry car No 2, which seated
22 passengers, was bought for £272 from Southern Railway in 1934.
WC&PR obtained quite a useful mileage from it, particularly during holiday
seasons, right up to 1940, and, of course, the Drewry offered passengers a
much less punishing ride than did a Ford or Shefflex. In circumstances described a little further on the GWR disposed of Drewry car No 2 in September 1940, for scrap.

8 April 1939 (2)

8 April 1939: Complications at Clevedon, where ex-LB&SCR 'Terrier' No 4 was co-opted, for some reason, to assist. No 4, formerly LB&SCR No 53 *Ashstead*, was purchased from the Southern Railway for £800 in 1937, twelve years after WC&PR acquired its first 'Terrier'. The latter, now W&CPR No 2, was given the name *Portishead*, but No 4 was never so honoured.

On went Le Manquais, grinding his way along this remarkable little railway, with its twenty stations and halts. It must have seemed a fascinating, albeit tiring, 14½ miles; and no doubt he was glad to stretch his legs at Portishead, WC&PR's northern terminus.

8 April 1939 (3)

8 April 1939: Portishead station, seen here from the north, looks very trim in the afternoon sunshine as a one-coach train awaits despatch back to Weston. The water tower on the right was a comparatively sophisticated Stephens innovation which automatically filled itself by electric pump. The line in the foreground carried on through level crossing gates to make connection with the GWR station at Portishead. The presence of Clee Hill Quarry wagons on the left implies a reasonably healthy exchange traffic with the GWR and presumably these have come all the way from Bitterley, where granite was brought down Clee Hill via a cable-worked 1¼-mile incline. A five-mile branch of the old Shrewsbury & Hereford Railway then took the wagons on to Ludlow.

8 April 1939: This fine study, Le Manquais' last WC&PR photograph, sums up quite poignantly the spirit of Colonel Stephens and his light railways. The four-wheeled coach (WC&PR No 18) is ex-Taff Vale Railway No 4021; though locomotive No 5, a Manning Wardle 0–6–0ST (Works No

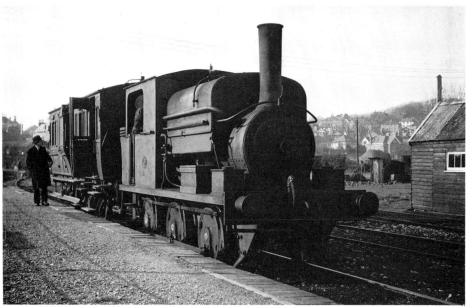

8 April 1939 (4)

1970/1919) was acquired in practically new condition in 1919. After many years of faithful service the little saddle tank, with its distinctive disc wheels, was sold on to industrial use in 1940.

Meanwhile, all is normal at Portishead. The train crew wait patiently inside their cab, and, familiar sight, a prospective passenger hesitates before taking the plunge.

When war broke out in 1939 the WC&PR was not one of those railways selected for national control by the Ministry of Transport. By now the line had not made a profit for thirty years, and Excess Insurance Co, anxious to disburden themselves, obtained a court order to close it. Thus, despite local protest, the WC&PR's last train ran on 18 May 1940. One month later the Ministry approved coal wagon storage on WC&PR metals, whence Paddington bought the system for £10,000. Everything passed into GWR ownership—and only two 'Terriers' survived. In the event very few wagons were ever stored: in 1942 track lifting operations commenced. They ultimately yielded 16,000 tons of steel, all of it useful wartime salvage. The real irony was that most of the track had been supplied in the first place by Krupps—of Essen . . .

CHAPTER NINE

Miscellaneous Observations

Miscellaneous, forsooth! Had space permitted, this chapter, the shortest in the book, might easily have been the longest, could I but have pursued the full range of Le Manquais' extraneous railway interests. For sheer perspicacity, coupled with an instinctive empathy for the 'off beat', led that gentleman into many an obscure corner, both at home and abroad.

Right from the start of his photographic career indications keep manifesting themselves of his highly informed curiosity. Away back in June 1929, for instance, the marshalling yards at Feltham occupied his attention for a full afternoon. A few days later, somewhere near St Helier, he could not resist a quick 'shot' from a carriage window as his Wimbledon-Sutton train passed an 825-acre LCC building site which was later to house 40,000 people. A network of flat-bottomed rail, supported by cinder ballast, had been laid to facilitate transfer of building materials—and there, tottering along in the near distance at the head of a few contractor's wagons, was Hunslet 0–6–0ST *Lionheart*! The picture, as it transpired, was not up to much; but the photographer's future intentions had been expressed clearly enough! The following spring, prowling round the Waddon Marsh area, he tracked down an intriguing cluster of ex-LB&SCR upper-quadrant signals. Then he wandered inquisitively on, west of the line, towards the gates of Croydon Gasworks. As luck would have it, he hardly needed to venture inside to find what he was looking for.

24 May 1930: Croydon Gas, Commercial & Coke Company, at its works near Waddon Marsh, acquired some interesting locomotives in its day; not least an Aveling Porter in 1901. Sentinel engine *Joyce*, seen here, was a worthy

24 May 1930

successor. Its vertical side-fired boiler could generate a tractive effort of 15,500 lb at speeds up to 1¼ mph. The water tank held 600 gallons, and 12 cwt of coal was stored in the bunker on the left hand side of the boiler. Coal, of course, was not a difficult commodity to locate at Croydon Gasworks; for the place received train loads of the stuff daily—until the intervention of road haulage and a rundown of conventional gas production coincided around 1967.

Two similar Sentinels, incidentally, were supplied to Somerset & Dorset Railway in 1929. Employed on colliery shunting, it was found they could perform a good day's work on 8–9 cwt of coal, half that consumed by ordinary shunting locomotives.

At that time Croydon was a particularly interesting locality. Thereby, in fact, hangs a tale; for, as I write, a vintage postcard of East Croydon Station lies before me. The view is readily identifiable as 'late 1920s', for catenaries of the Brighton-type overhead electric system the Southern Railway initially installed are well in evidence. Clearly visible, too, are the prominently advertised premises of Hall & Co— 'Established 1842. Coal & Gravel. Builders' Merchants'. Indeed, the only puzzling element is the identity of a small locomotive which is shunting on a short siding adjacent thereto. Viewed distantly, and from the rear, the loco's foursquare aspect suggests it might be a Sentinel shunter. Yet irrefutable evidence of a canopy roof, and a stovepipe chimney up front, dispels that theory. What on earth, then, was it! For years I speculated on the subject, and got no further. Then, one day, Le Manquais' negatives and notebooks arrived on the scene, and—hey presto, *there* was the answer!

14 April 1931: Twice, once in 1896 and again in 1915, J&H McLaren's Midland Engine Works at Leeds deviated briefly from normal production of gas and oil engines to build a small steam locomotive of the traction engine type. The 1915 engine (Works No 1547) is seen here in Hall & Co's private

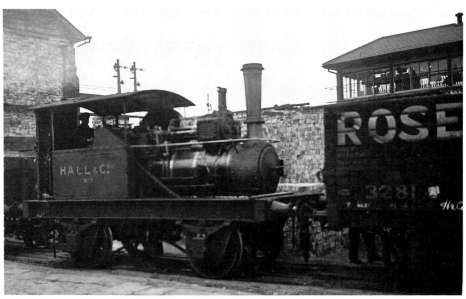

14 April 1931

yard. Numbered 9, it was a compound, with cylinders 6½in × 10¾in × 12in, and with wagon-type wheels, 3ft 1in diameter. The Croydon firm, which employed a fair number of steam locomotives in its day, evidently placed some credence on the use of traction engines; for, fifty years earlier, it purchased two four-wheeled specimens of the genre from Clayton Shuttleworth & Co's Stamp End Works at Lincoln.

East Croydon's main line signalbox lies behind in this interesting study.

Midway between his local discoveries Le Manquais also took pains to visit Wantage, the Oxfordshire home of Britain's most famous roadside steam tramway. The latter was opened in October 1875 as a desirable link between the town of Wantage and GWR's Wantage Road Station, 2¾ miles away. Inevitably, however, Wantage Tramway experienced the usual vicissitudes of light railway fortune: the twin pressures of financial stringency and bus competition forced withdrawal of passenger services in 1925. The question was now, as Le Manquais well knew—how much longer would freight traffic linger on?

Omens as he approached Wantage Town yard that afternoon were not propitious; for the only visible sign of life came from locomotive No 7, a Manning Wardle 0–4–0ST (Works No 1057/1888). Theoretically, it was engaged in shunting a few wagons; but, significantly, neither driver nor fireman was averse to stopping for a photograph or two. That done, the whereabouts of the only other surviving Wantage engine, 0–4–0WT No 5, built by George England & Co, originally for the Sandy & Potton Railway, in 1857, was soon established. *It*, if you please, was sleeping soundly inside the tramway's modest wooden shed! Obviously, there was no scope there for a camera; so Le Manquais transferred his attention to an open siding nearby. There, completely exposed to the elements, he found the saddest sight of all— the last remnants of Wantage Tramway's finest hours.

26 September 1930

26 September 1930: Memories of passenger traffic long, long gone are evoked by this spectacle of steam tram No 6 mouldering away in a siding at Wantage Town, in company with cars Nos 5 and 4. While considerable controversy still exists as to who built the tram locomotive, we know that it was bought by Wantage Tramway Co Ltd in 1885, and functioned as their No 6 until passenger traffic ceased on 31 July 1925. The wheels were situated between the frames, but were not coupled. Thus, despite the orthodox positioning of outside cylinders and valve gear, tram No 6 ran as a 2–2–0. Car No 5, seen on the right, was a four-wheeled ex-Reading horse tram vehicle. Its partner, No 4, off right, was bogied.

In the event Wantage freight services limped gallantly on through the 1930s. Then came World War 2, and subsequent harsh treatment of tramway metals by American Army vehicles made recovery so impossible that the seventy-year-old concern was closed, by Ministry of Transport Order, on 21 December 1945. Dissolution was swift. The two steam locos along with three miles of track etc, were put up for auction, and No 7, repaired at Swindon as recently as 1944, went to Messrs Adams of Newport, Mon. Overhauled and resold, it eventually found re-employment at Corde Steel Mills in that town.

Twelve months later a fortuitous trip north saw Le Manquais add a second pioneer railway to his collection. This one, though, had a vastly different pedigree.

All through the mid-19th century the problem of severe railway congestion along the length and breadth of Liverpool Docks exercised the minds of authority. 1886 arrived, however, before Mersey Docks & Harbour Board obtained Parliamentary sanction to construct an elevated passenger railway based on that already established in New York. There was, though, to be one vital difference. New York used steam: Liverpool, after some indecision, opted for electric traction. Thus was

born the Liverpool Overhead Railway, the world's first overhead electric railway. A five-mile section, embracing thirteen stations, was opened on 6 March 1893.

Constructional problems were formidable; for the standard-gauge track ran practically its full length along a steel viaduct pitched some 16ft above ground level. Three lifting bridges and a swing bridge had to be incorporated to permit passage below of high loads after normal railway working hours, and three bow girder bridges, each 95ft long, were also required. In all 20,000 tons of iron and steel were consumed. Capital costs soared accordingly to £90,000 per mile. Thirty motor coaches, to be used in dual formation, were provided for the 1893 opening; and, so successful was the railway that provision of additional trailer cars two years later saw three-car operation firmly established. Extensions, north and south, in 1894–96 added seven stations and just under two route miles of track; while, in 1905, a further double line connection near Seaforth Sands ushered in through running with L&YR's electrically-worked Liverpool–Southport branch.

22 August 1931 (1)

22 August 1931: Passing through one of three bow girder bridges which spanned wide streets in the vicinity, motor coach No 45, supplied by Brown Marshall & Co in 1895, leads a standard three-car train through morning mist into Pier Head, Liverpool Overhead Railway's busiest station. Note the watertight metal decking, the 'Dockers' Umbrella', which protected general activity 16ft below; also the train stop sited between the tracks. Automatic colour light signalling, the first of its type in the country, was introduced in 1921, and throughout the 1930s six million passengers were carried each year. World War 2 air raid damage and post-war bus competition, however, proved lethal and after more than sixty years of service Liverpool's unique overhead railway ran its last train on Sunday, 30 December 1956.

The LOR was undeniably a great asset to Liverpool's dockers. But quite early in the century a vigorous publicity campaign waged by its management also urged the public at large not to miss LOR's 'magnificent 6½-mile panoramic view of Liverpool Docks. Trains every five minutes'. Thus, with a ringside view of mighty Atlantic liners thrown in as an added attraction, a peak figure of 19 million passengers was reached in 1919.

Meanwhile, in the midst of all this exclusively electrical activity one lone steam engine soldiered quietly on: a tiny 0–4–0WT, bought new from Kitson & Co in 1893, it found regular employment at the hands of LOR's Engineers Department, usually after normal traffic hours, and rejoiced in the nickname of 'Lively Polly'. Almost incredibly, Le Manquais ran *it* to ground as well!

22 August 1931 (2)

22 August 1931: When Seaforth Sands Station was resited in 1926, and a new carriage shed was built on the old station site, a small shed was also provided for Liverpool Overhead Railway's solitary steam locomotive. This view, taken from the new station's platforms, offers only a tantalizing glimpse of the shed's contents. 'Lively Polly' can just be seen on the right, and next, behind the stepladder, lies a breakdown tool van. One of the LOR Engineers Department four-wheeled, two-seater pedal track cycles can also be spotted.

Once a Ruston diesel, purchased in August 1947, took over Departmental duties, 'Lively Polly' was sold. Subsequently overhauled at Wrexham by Messrs Cudworth & Johnson, it finished its days working on Rea Limited's coal wharf at Birkenhead.

Pausing long enough to enjoy a week's respite in the Lake District, Le Manquais next contrived somehow to collect a second electric railway scalp; this time in the Manchester vicinity.

29 August 1931

29 August 1931: The Manchester, South Junction & Altrincham Railway, opened on 21 July 1869, relied on steam for over sixty years. Latterly it was worked and supervised alternately by a GCR and LNWR Joint Committee. Then came Grouping, and the nominally independent railway passed into LMSR and LNER joint ownership. Electric traction took over on 11 May 1931; whence stopping trains were scheduled to complete the 8¾ miles between Manchester (London Road) and Altrincham in 24 minutes. Initial provision of 24 motor coaches, 22 trailers, and 22 driving trailer coaches was made by Metropolitan Cammell. A sub-station at Stretford provided 1,500 volts DC for the overhead wire system, and 125 trains ran six days a week on this busy line. The non-stop express seen here passing Stretford consisted of a double set of normal three-coach compartmented trains.

In 1941, when the LNER decided to electrify its Sheffield-Manchester route, prototype electric locomotive No 6701 was tested over the MSJ&AR line. Steam services from Manchester (Central) and (London Road) to Northwich and Liverpool respectively also used these metals; the latter until 1962. Today they still support quite an intensive diesel-hauled freight traffic.

By now Le Manquais' keen interest in electric railways, truly a premonstration of his later occupation in life, was so self-evident that it could only be a matter of time before the name Magnus Volk would lure him to Brighton. Surely enough, that mission was accomplished the day he visited the West Sussex Light Railway at Chichester.

Brighton-born in 1851 of German parents, Magnus Volk introduced electric light to his home town at the age of thirty. With Corporation permission he then built a ¼-mile 2ft gauge electric public tramway along the sea front, between Aquarium and the old Chain Pier. Current, generated by a gas engine and Siemens dynamo housed in a retaining wall, was fed to two flat-bottomed running rails, spiked to longitudinal wooden sleepers. A four-wheeled car, built locally, served to accommodate both motor and ten passengers. Amidst great excitement, Volk's Electric Railway was opened to the public on 4 August 1883—it was an immediate success.

Heartened thus, Volk closed the line briefly in January 1884 to convert it over the next three months to 2ft 9in gauge. Half a mile longer by dint of an extension to Paston Place, it reopened on 4 April 1884 with two new double-ended cars. A regular 5–6 minute service, summer and winter, ensued from that day to 2 July 1940, with only occasional interruption from gales. During the 1890s a third off-centre rail was installed, gauge was reduced to 2ft 8½in, and further extension to Black Rock brought total length to 1¾ miles. A year later traction current was drawn from Brighton Corporation's electric mains.

26 September 1933

26 September 1933: West of Paston Place, at the approach to Aquarium Station, Volk's Electric Railway swept above beach level and ran along a miniature viaduct above the shingle. Here the sea came under at high tide, and many a storm swamped passing cars in spray. In a moment the left hand of the driver of this 'Toastrack' car will reach towards the roof, where lay his speed control switch. Mercifully, this remarkable pioneer railway, though closed during World War 2 for security reasons, still functions under Borough of Brighton auspices, and recently celebrated its centenary. All through its long history it maintained a tradition of heavy holiday traffic, and even as late as 1955 it handled 775,000 passengers. Before buses ran in competition along the front the figure was nearer one million.

We close this book, reluctantly but appropriately enough, by reproducing the last photograph Le Manquais took before the events of 3 September 1939 obliged him, and the rest of us, to abandon photography *sine die*. Rather remarkably, in light of war tremors which were disturbing Central Europe at the time, he and his wife left Parkeston Quay on a prolonged Scandinavian holiday on 22 July 1939. Landing at

Esbjerg, they enjoyed a totally successful three-week tour of Denmark, Sweden and Norway, before re-embarking at Stavanger on SS *Venus*. Railway and general scenes there continued to occupy his camera, as they had done all through his holiday. Nevertheless, in the circumstances, one can imagine Le Manquais' feeling of relief once he and his wife set foot again on English soil.

13 August 1939

13 August 1939: Sunday at Newcastle Tyne Commission Quay, and, headed temporarily by ex-NER 'H5' Class 0–4–4T No 2086, the LNER's through restaurant car train, 'The Norseman', is ready to leave at 1.40 pm. Proceeding *via* Newcastle (Central), it will reach King's Cross at 8.27 pm. This unusual service was reserved for boat passengers, and, running on Tuesdays, Thursdays, Fridays, and Sundays only, it awaited B&N Line steamers' arrival from Bergen.

   Three weeks after this photograph was taken Britain and Germany were at war.

I mentioned earlier that Le Manquais calmly used up the unexpired portion of that film five years later, in June 1944. As one who has been tempted more than once in the past to indulge in out-of-date film 'bargains', I am bound to raise an understanding hat. But I am even more bound to confess that my admiration for Le Manquais' sheer self-discipline increased to a new dimension when I discovered, written in his notebook, after that five-year-old film had been developed for sixteen laborious minutes, the gentle, but unmistakably self-admonishing, inscription—'Rather undeveloped?'

   Typical, was it not?

   Rest in peace, my friend . . .

INDEX

(Page numbers in *italics* refer to illustrations)